Labouring Side by Side

The Local Church as the Most Significant Arena for Evangelism and Disciple-Making

by
Dr. John Wesley Zwomunondiita Kurewa

Africa Ministry Series

DISCIPLESHIP RESOURCES
— INTERNATIONAL —

Labouring Side by Side

The Local Church as the Most Significant Arena for Evangelism and Disciple-Making
Copyright © 2011 Discipleship Resources International. All rights reserved.

Cover and interior design: Karin Wizer
Cover photo: Jeff Oliver
Typesetting: PerfecType, Nashville, TN

ISBN 978-0-88177-869-4

Contents

Preface

The ministry of evangelism is at its best when it occurs in and through the local church, and when it is experienced by members at the local church level. *The Book of Discipline of the United Methodist Church* puts it aptly when it says, "The local church provides the most significant arena through which disciple-making occurs."[1] If the church was to be considered as a manufacturing company, the local church would be its production floor, for this is the place where lives of many people are transformed. It is at the local church level that people have made meaningful commitments to Christ or have had conversion experiences; it is also here that newly converted Christians are nurtured and enabled to move onto a path of continuous growth in their Christian faith. It is at the local church level that Christians often discover their potential and become obedient to being commissioned as witnesses for Christ, both in their communities and in the world. It is through nurture by the local church that Christians often learn to distinguish between the voice of the Good Shepherd and those of strangers. When they know the voice of the Good Shepherd, they easily run away from following the strangers—false prophets, false spiritual healers, and other strange voices. Because they know the voice of their Shepherd, they will always respond to and follow him (John 10:4ff), for he alone is "the way and the truth and the life" (John 14:6).

As leaders in African local churches, we read much about different and new ways of doing evangelism from Asia, from Latin America, and from western churches—our mother churches. All that knowledge may enrich and bless our mind and soul. Still, as the church in Africa, we need to experience the ministry of evangelism primarily as it occurs and is experienced by Africans today. It is not only a question of indigenization; rather it is also an issue of contextualization of the gospel to the local communities. This book takes seriously the idea of African local churches localizing the ministry of evangelism, for that is the best arena for converts to make their commitment to Jesus Christ and to be nurtured and guided toward Christian maturity. Further, it is the best arena for evangelism in the sense that the pastor labours side by side with the members of the congregation—enabling the laity to learn what their clergy know about evangelism.

It was no accident that when God sought to establish God's kingdom on earth through God's Son, God began the whole process by localizing Jesus in our midst, as John reports: "The Word became flesh and made his dwelling among us. We have seen his glory, the glory of the One and Only, who came from the Father, full of grace and truth" (John 1:14).

The Son himself confirmed the idea when he told his disciples that after they have received the power from the Holy Spirit, they would become Jesus' witnesses "in Jerusalem, and in all Judea and Samaria, and to the ends of the earth" (Acts 1:8). It all began with the local church congregation of Jerusalem.

The thesis of this book is that the local church provides the most significant arena through which disciple-making occurs. This is a point that needs to be understood by all who share in the administration of the church and those who are appointed to share in the ministry of leading the local churches, circuits, and parishes into God's mission. It also follows that if the local church provides the most significant arena through which disciple-making occurs, the local church needs greater attention than we are giving it today. The local church is where most people commit their lives to Christ, and where the people receive their religious education regarding who they are as new humanity in Christ. The local church is where this new humanity in Christ is challenged to take up God's mission and assume its responsibility in communities throughout the world. What is needed for the local church to accomplish its mission? The pastor in a local church needs adequate training to lead and to train; the laity need training for the doctrine of the ministry of all believers to fully function. And more money may need to be spent on the local church so that it will be able to commission more and more people to realize the mission of God in our communities.

The content of the materials presented in the following chapters have been prepared with the local churches of Africa in mind. Chapter 1 gives the historical background of the various terms that refer to the basic, or smallest, organizational structure of the church. Chapter 2 explains the meaning of the gospel that Christians share with others, and evangelism as a ministry of the church that focuses on the spreading of that gospel to others. In Chapter 3 we discuss the importance of the ministry of all believers. Chapter 4 discusses evangelism as the mission of the local church. Chapters 5 and 6 are modified reprints from my book *Drumbeats of Salvation in Africa* (Africa University Press, 2007).

This book is directed to the members of local churches who often lack access to reading materials on the ministry of evangelism, and especially for those who think evangelism is only for gifted persons, or only for pastors. This book could be used as a study guide by any group of a local church that seeks to be effective in the ministry of evangelism in its community.

Chapter 1

What Is the Local Church?

The term *local church* may not be used universally. Different denominations use various terms to refer to the smallest church unit of a people who worship together from time to time. Other terms that various churches use may be considered as equivalent though with variations in meaning. An understanding of the historical background of these terms will broaden our understanding of the task under our consideration, namely, evangelism through the local church. These terms are as follows: *congregation, parish, circuit,* and *the local church.*

Defining the Local Church

First, *congregation*: After their Egypt experience, the children of Israel became aware for the first time of the potential of their oneness; they became conscious of being one people—a *congregation* in the desert and the ensuing purpose that the "the people of Israel were considered as a group for *travel*" (see Exod. 16:1).[2] This same idea is expressed within the Zimbabwe Episcopal Area of The United Methodist Church as *Tiriparwendo*, which means "we are on a journey," a journey of faith or a pilgrimage. Later, Israel is also considered as a group for *worship*[3] and also as *sacred assemblies*, and according to the Septuagint translated *ecclesia*,[4] meaning church. Thus in some church traditions the local church is referred to as a *congregation.*

Second, *parish*: In the Middle Ages (950–1350), the bishop was more than just an administrator of the church. He was in charge of worship and supervised the entire life of the church in the town and the surrounding area. The territorial area that one bishop supervised became known as a *diocese*. In some areas, notably in North Africa and Italy, every town had its own bishop. However, further territorial subdivisions took place, creating what came to be known as *parishes*, which were under the charge of a presbyter or priest who was supervised by a bishop.[5] The parish system was well established in the Frankish domains (the West Germanic language or culture of the Franks), even in the countryside. And each parish had its priest. The parishes and chapels were endowed with lands by local magnates (influential persons, or businessmen) "for 'the salvation of their souls'. But the donors retained for themselves and their heirs the privilege of naming the pastors"[6] rather than the bishop appointing pastors. The *parish* was the unit around which activities of the local population revolved—baptisms, marriages, and mass. And "mass was supposed to be said daily."[7] In the medieval period mass was served three times in a day. A parish could consist of one or more *local churches*.

Third, *circuit*: The term *circuit* belongs to Methodism. "The unit of the organization is the local church or 'charge' as it has always been called in Methodism."[8] After John Wesley organized the societies, he subdivided those societies into circuits. At first the circuits were very large and gradually they were reduced in size as the movement advanced. After 1748, representatives of each society in the circuit met once a quarter.[9] Hence the meetings became known as *quarterly conferences*. Wesley remained the superintendent of the circuits, although he also appointed assistant superintendents to each of the circuits.[10] It became customary that a preacher would stay in the circuit for three years, as Wesley "calculated that a preacher would have preached to the same congregation all that he usefully could in about three years."[11] The practice of calling his clerical supporters and his preachers to what became an *annual conference* to settle the main affairs of the Connexion began in 1745.[12] Thus, the pastor would plan his/her work on the basis of *a circuit*, although it may consist of a number of local churches.

Fourth, *local church*: According to *The Book of Discipline of the United Methodist Church*:

It |the local church| is the redemptive fellowship in which the Word of God is preached by persons divinely called and the sacraments are duly administered according to Christ's own appointment. Under the discipline of the Holy Spirit, the church exists for the maintenance of the worship, the edification of believers, and the redemption of the world.[13]

We have already noted that *The Book of Discipline of The United Methodist Church* acknowledges, "The local church provides the most significant arena through which disciple-making occurs." Bryan Green, a great priest-evangelist who became known as Canon of Birmingham in England in the 1950s, defined the local church as "a local community of worshipping believers who in present day conditions meet and worship in one given centre."[14] Thus, we could also define the local church as the church that we attend every Sunday, or whatever day and time when we are called to worship together.

Members of the Local Church

Every local church/circuit/parish or congregation has its members. These are the people that this book is concerned with. These members of local churches are the people considered as our ministers or priests, and they have ministries to perform for Christ in whatever local church they belong. The membership of a local United Methodist church includes those who have been baptized and those who have professed their faith.[15] To join a church, or become a member in The United Methodist Church means to be in fellowship with all other believers, as The United Methodist Church is part of the Church Universal.[16] The success of any local church in achieving its goals of mission depends on its ability to be mobilized as a congregation, a local church, a parish, or a circuit for that mission.

Chapter 2

What Is Evangelism?

It is important to state at the outset that the terms *evangelism* and *the gospel* are intricately related to the extent that some Christians mistakenly use the two terms interchangeably. Indeed, the terms both come from the Greek word *euaggelion* or *evangel*, which means *good news* or *message*.[17] The term *evangel* was translated into old English as *godspel*, meaning *good news*; it comes to us as *gospel*.[18] However, while *gospel* means message or good news, *evangelism* means sharing or communicating that message or good news. To say it another way, *gospel* refers to the substance to be shared; *evangelism* refers to the activity of sharing the gospel.

Defining the Gospel

Paul defines the gospel as follows:

> Paul, a servant of Christ Jesus, called to be an apostle and set apart *for the gospel of God*—the gospel he promised beforehand through his prophets in the holy Scriptures *regarding his* Son, who as to his human nature was a descendent of David, and who through the Spirit of holiness was declared with power to be *the Son of God* by his resurrection from the dead; *Jesus Christ our Lord.* (Rom. 1:1–4, italics mine)

For Paul, God the Father set him apart from birth and called him by grace so that he would preach *Jesus Christ* among the Gentiles (Gal.

1:16). From prison Paul wrote to strengthen his son of faith Timothy, "Remember *Jesus Christ*, raised from the dead, descended from David. This is my *gospel*, for which I am suffering, even to the point of being chained like a criminal. *But God's word is not chained*" (2 Tim. 2:8–9, italics mine). Thus in all the above texts, Paul defined the gospel as Jesus Christ, hence writing to the Corinthians, ". . . we preach *Christ crucified*" (1 Cor. 1:23, italics mine).

John defines the gospel in this manner, "That which was from the beginning, which we have heard, which we have seen with our eyes, which we have looked at and our hands have touched—this we proclaim concerning the Word of life" (1 John 1:1). John is trying to show that the one who always existed with the eternal Father actually became flesh, that is, human; and that he, Jesus Christ, was true God and truly man. He was their gospel, and he was the one that John and others proclaimed (1 John 1:3).

In the accounts of both Paul and John, the gospel is *Jesus Christ*. He is the one the apostles proclaimed to the world; he is the good news to the world.

Defining Evangelism

We have already said that while *gospel* refers to the substance to be communicated or shared, *evangelism* is the ministry of communicating or sharing that gospel. Evangelism refers to *evangelizing* or *gospelizing* or communicating Jesus Christ to others—that is, introducing other people to Jesus Christ. I often prefer defining evangelism in a four-fold manner:

a. *Evangelism is one of the ministries of the church.* It deserves the same attention as worship and music, Christian education, Christian social concerns, and stewardship.

b. *Evangelism is the heart of evangelization,*[19] *or the mission of the church.* It is the heartbeat ministry of the local church. A human being who

14

no longer has a heartbeat is dead. So it is with a local church that no longer experiences the ministry of evangelism. The joy of witnessing conversions in the congregation and the community is gone and the joyous celebration of new converts joining the church ceases. It was about such a church, the church of Laodicea, that the Lord said through John on the island of Patmos, "I know your deeds, that you are neither cold nor hot. I wish your were either one or the other! So, because you are lukewarm—neither hot nor cold—I am about to spit you out of my mouth" (Rev. 3:15–16). A local church must maintain its heartbeat ministry—evangelism.

    c. *The focus of evangelism as a ministry of the church is sharing or communicating to others the gospel—Jesus Christ (in word and deed).*

    d. *Evangelism is best conducted through a local church.* Local churches are the best arena, as opposed to wandering evangelists. A local church can secure people's commitment to Christ; it can guide newly converted persons in their Christian growth; and can guide "them in discovering the implications of their life together in the church and in the world."[20]

Quoting from David Barrett's booklet, *Evangelize,* Walter Klaiber, a retired Methodist Bishop of Germany and a New Testament scholar, reminds us of the two schools of thought in evangelism. For the first school of thought, to evangelize is "to preach, bring, tell, proclaim, announce, or declare the Gospel . . . whether the people accept it or not, whether they are then won or converted by the activity or not, although this is the intent."[21] This definition of evangelism "corresponds to the language use of the New Testament, and is used by exegetes, Christian lexicographers [a person who writes or compiles a dictionary], and missiologists."[22]

John Stott, who supports the same position, points out that evangelism must not be defined in "terms of its results, for this is not how the word is used in the New Testament"[23] (see Acts 8:4; 14:7; Romans 15:20).[24] Neither should evangelism be defined in terms of methods. For example, some people define evangelism as "the proclamation of the gospel" (proclamation is a method of evangelism). According to this school of thought, evangelism "must be defined in terms of the *message*."[25] D. T. Niles is said to have defined evangelism as one beggar telling another beggar where to find bread. Whether the other beggar goes on to help himself/herself or not, the *message* or *good news* has been communicated. So it is with evangelism for the first school of thought. Christ must be shared with others. If those who hear the message decide not to receive it, the messenger cannot be blamed.

For the second school of thought of evangelism, Klaiber says that to evangelize is "not just to proclaim, but to actually win and convert people to the Christian faith."[26] Preaching practitioners of evangelism, non-theological dictionaries, and the majority of Christians use this second meaning.[27] This concept of evangelism seems to be more common among our Christians and churches in Africa. Some hold this view to an extreme at times and tend to think that each time they share the gospel with someone, those persons must always accept Christ. Those who hold this belief, whether evangelists or pastors, seem to be forcing people to become converts.

There are two things to remember, regardless of the school of thought to which one belongs. First, it is God who converts people; a pastor or evangelist does not. In exhorting his disciples, Jesus made this point when he talked about the coming of the Holy Spirit, "When he comes, he will convict the world of guilt in regard to sin and righteousness and judgment" (John 16:8). Paul states the same message, though differently, when he says to the Corinthian church, it is "God who makes things grow" (1 Cor. 3:7). God gives life. God is the one who brings about new life in a person. Second, in the task of evangelism, or in the conversion of people, the role of the pastor or evangelist is like that of a planter and waterer. "I planted the seed, Apollos watered it, but God made it grow" (1 Cor. 3:6).

However, the role of the pastor or pastor-evangelist in evangelism is not merely explaining all that God can do for people. Rather, it is also being conscious of the fact that, through our preaching and sharing of Christ, God may communicate caring love and mercy to the people. For "revelation is not something within our personal power, it is the concern of God."[28] In spite of all human limitations, the fact is that God may choose to work through our human efforts. It is a privilege and blessing that God can use people like us as "an instrument for noble purposes" (2 Tim. 2:21). A pastor or a member of the church becomes God's fellow worker, God's partner, as God reaches out to God's people (1 Cor. 3:9). What a blessing in one's life!

Chapter 3

Ministry of All Believers

A local church determined to take the ministry of evangelism seriously in its community and in the world will need to acknowledge
the enormous power within the laity and each member of the church.
This acknowledgement is wielded in the doctrine of the ministry of all
believers or priesthood of all believers. The concept can be traced back
to the time of Moses, when Moses and the children of Israel camped
in the desert of Sinai, where the Lord called to Moses from the mountain and said these words about the children of Israel, "Although the
whole earth is mine, you will be for me a kingdom of priests and a
holy nation" (Exod. 19:5–6). Later, in Isaiah, the Lord refers to Israel as
". . . my people, my chosen, the people I formed for myself that they may
proclaim my praise" (Isaiah 43:20–21). Hence, in New Testament times,
Peter wrote to local churches scattered throughout Pontus, Galatia,
Cappadocia, Asia, and Bithynia, ". . . you are a chosen people, a royal
priesthood, a holy nation, a people belonging to God" (1 Pet. 2:9).

The Old Testament refers to Israel as "the kingdom of priests and a
holy nation." "My people, my chosen," were terms adopted by Peter for
Christian usage. He perceived the scattered Christian communities as
a chosen people, a royal priesthood, a holy nation, a people belonging
to God. He saw them as people who, as a new Israel, not only had
direct access to Christ, but who would also minister to others, including through prayer to God, regardless of their geographical location or
station in life. He urged those Christian communities to acknowledge
their role as priests among the people and in the communities where
they found themselves.

Meaning of Ministry of All Believers

Ministry or priesthood of all believers is "the phrase symbolic of one of the basic and distinctive principles of Protestant Reformation."[29] According to Martin Luther (1483–1546), the meaning of ministry of all believers is: (a) that every Christian has direct access to Christ; and (b) that all Christians are "worthy to appear before God to pray for others and teach one another the things of God."[30] For Luther, this also meant that every Christian is a priest, and a servant of all. At the same time Luther rejected the medieval tradition that identified the priesthood with the sacraments, and the conception that the priesthood constitutes a special class in the eyes of God.

One day as I passed through one of the cities in the United States, I came to a church where the sign out front read: "In this congregation we have 500 ministers and one pastor." I interpreted that to mean that the five hundred members of the church included full members and probationary members, who by virtue of confessing Christ had automatically joined the royal priesthood of Christ. The ministry or the priesthood of all believers is an important doctrine for the church to know, to practice, and to instruct all members of the local church.

Its Origin in the Early Church

The first followers of Jesus were known as *disciples* (Acts 6:1, 7; 9:1, 19, 26; 14:20, 22). The name *disciple* included everyone who followed or was baptized in the name of Jesus. At some point those disciples became known as "people who belonged to the Way" (Acts 9:2; 24:14), for Jesus is the *way* to the Father (John 14:6). That means the disciples' faith in Jesus was "considered as *the way* of life or *the way* of salvation."[31] It was from Antioch that for the first time those disciples of Jesus became known as *Christians* (Acts 11:26). They were disciples, they were a people of the way, and they were Christians.

20

Those early Christians understood themselves as a people who had received the divine *calling* or *call* (*klesis*) to salvation (Rom. 8:30; 11:29; 1 Cor. 1:26; 7:20; Eph. 1:18; 4:1, 4; Phil. 3:14; 2 Thess. 1:11; 2 Tim. 1:9; Heb. 3:1; 2 Pet. 1:10).[32] That was a divine *call* to partake of the blessings of redemption (Rom. 8:30; 1 Cor. 1:9; 1 Thess. 2:12; Heb. 9:15).[33] The call was to follow Jesus, and those who accepted the call were baptized in Jesus' name and became his disciples, or Christians. The early church associated that divine calling with Christian discipleship.

They also perceived themselves as the body of Christ (1 Cor. 12:27; Eph. 4:12), or one body in Christ (Rom.12:5). Paul puts it eloquently when he says, "Just as each one of us has one body with many members, and these members do not all have the same function, so in Christ we who are many form one body, and each member belongs to all the others" (Rom. 12:4–5). However, that one body, or the church, of Christ was endowed with a "diversity of gifts" that included the message of wisdom, the message of knowledge, faith, healing, miraculous powers, prophecy, distinguishing between spirits, speaking in different kinds of tongues, and the interpretation of tongues (1 Cor. 12:12–31a). To the church in Rome the gifts are presented as "individual talents" of prophesying, serving, teaching, encouraging, contributing to the needs of others, leadership, and showing mercy (Rom. 12:6–8).

The point is that every member of the church has been given a gift that each is expected to use to the fullest potential. Because these gifts are different, one is not supposed to think of his or her gift as more important than that of the other. Hence, the illustration of how members of the body function, each in its own way, yet for the common ministry. Those are all spiritual gifts, or talents, along with many others that we may find in members of our local churches today. However, those early Christians used those spiritual gifts or talents for the glory of God. A statement by Bruce Larson makes an interesting point when he says, "In its first 300 years of history, the church had no clergy. Rather, it was made up of believers who understood they were to be apostles, sent on mission by the living Christ."[34]

A significant fact concerning the early church is that it thrived under harsh and severe measures of persecution by the Roman emperors. Such murderous persecution was inflicted on Jesus of Nazareth who suffered death under Pontius Pilate, prefect or governor of Judea around 30 CE. Having raised Jesus from the dead, according to Peter's message on the day of Pentecost, God made Jesus "both Lord and Christ" (Acts 2:36). And as the number of Christian disciples increased in the Roman empire, persecution of Christians by the Roman emperors intensified. It began with the persecution of the church in Jerusalem, throughout Judea, Samaria, and the cities of neighbouring countries, such as Damascus following the stoning of Stephen (Acts 8, 9). In addition, Herod had James, brother of John, arrested and put to death by the sword (Acts 12:2). Nero's (54–68 CE) persecution took the lives of Peter and Paul in Rome, among others. Sporadic persecutions in the province of Asia Minor took the life of Polycarp, the bishop of Smyrna in Rome (156 CE), and the last survivor to have talked with the eyewitness of Jesus.[35] Marcus Aurelius (161–180) took the lives of many African Christians, such as Perpetua and Felicitas. Severus's persecution (193–197), Decius (249–251) and Valerian persecutions attacked leaders such as Cyprian, who lost his life.

That imperial persecution of Christians during the first three or four centuries CE had great impact on Christian communities, with differences from one place to another: (a) because Christian communities were an underground movement, they became primarily house churches; (b) a sense of oneness, both as individual communities and as the church universal, remained vital; they were the body of Christ with a diversity of gifts as Paul had expounded; and, (c) the believers made no difference in dress between the clergy and laity for such "distinction would have made the clergy conspicuous and would have singled them out for arrest."[36]

Its Decline in the Medieval Church

The division between clergy and laity was clearly established after Christianity became an official religion of the empire in 312 CE.

First, "probably early in 313 Constantine and Licinius met at Milan and came to some mutual agreement permitting full freedom to Christianity. This has generally been known as the *Edict of Milan*."[37] Thus, Christianity became an official religion of the Roman empire and enjoyed the same privileges as the royal Roman religion.

Second, the recognition of Christianity as an official religion was followed by massive construction of basilicas. In describing that transitional part of history, from the early to the medieval church, Samuel Laeuchli writes, "Out of the fanatic struggle an impressive era arose: vast basilicas, powerful Episcopal sees, worldwide theological debates, and a Christian population spanning the Mediterranean shores."[38]

Third, clerical attire developed in stages: (a) "At that time |4th and 5th century| the outdoor dress of the Roman civil officials was an undergarment, a tunic, with or without sleeves, and an immense sleeveless cloak which was without an opening in the front and was passed over the head. The undergarment might be bound around the waist by a girdle. . . (b) By the end of the fifth century a second tunic with large sleeves called the dalmatic, worn over the undergarment and under the cloak, became a distinguishing mark of the Pope and his clergy. . . (c) In the East, as early as the fourth century, bishops, priests and deacons had the *orarium*, a conventionalized form of handkerchief or neck-cloth. It was linen and was worn as a stole, draped over the shoulder."[39]

Fourth, although the Eucharist became central in medieval church worship, it also became a divisive factor between the clergy and laity. Reinhold Seeberg observed:

All the orders have a relation nearer or more remote to the Eucharist. The priest consecrates; the deacon is permitted to distribute the blood; the sub-deacon may bring the materials to be consecrated. The others are engaged in preparing for the reception of the sacrament.[40]

Howard Grimes quotes from the Constitution of the Holy Apostles II, probably from the early fourth century, where the lay person was exhorted:

To honour the bishop as to a good shepherd, to love him, reverence him as his lord, and his master, as the high priest of God, as a teacher of piety. . . the keeper of knowledge, the mediator between God and you in the several parts of your divine worship.[41]

The division between clergy and laity increased so that in the West the priest stood at communion, and the layman knelt; the priest partook of both elements, the laity, only of one.[42] Hendrik Kraemer, a Dutch theologian, regretted the division that he interprets as having happened by an accident of history to the extent that today the Church is divided between clergy and laity. He sees the clergy today as the rulers and administrators, almost at the exclusion of the laity. He sees the clergy ". . . as a rule, the spokesmen of the Church are considered to be the really authentic spokesmen."[43] What happened that the body of Christ became divided between the clergy and laity?

Fifth, soon the laity felt spiritual emptiness in their lives and began to pursue ascetic life. Some early ascetic movements such as Montanism (late 2nd, 3rd centuries) were declared heretical, but not all.[44] Monasticism originated in the third century and flourished as a lay movement. That was partly because laity had been shut out of participation in the life of the church as equal partners—"a royal priesthood of all believers." Kraemer points out again, "In the first four centuries, in many local congregations the laity exercised influence when a new bishop had to be elected. A very striking example is Augustine, who literally was forced to the episcopal seat by the congregation."[45]

Sixth, by contrast, the powers of the laity were also curtailed by the powerful clergy, as again, we note that Origen was the last charismatic independent and lay teacher. The bishops would not allow it any more. It was Cyprian, Bishop of Carthage (200–258), who drove the last nail when he taught that the unity of the Church was focused on the bishops:

> You ought to know that the bishop is in the church and the church is in the bishop. If any one is not with the bishop, he is not in the church. Bishops are the successors of the apostles, i.e. they take over the functions of the apostles. The bishop is supreme in his own church, though he remains a bishop only in solidarity with the other bishops of the Catholic Church.[46]

The clergy succeeded in taking over the rule and spokesmanship of the church of Christ.

Its Revival in the Reformation of the Church

The leading reformers claimed the ministry of all believers as embedded in the early church. They realized the medieval church had distorted the perception of this ministry and sought to revive it. For our purpose, we shall select reformers Martin Luther (1483–1546) and Philip Jacob Spener (1675–1705) and examine their views on the ministry or the priesthood of all believers. Martin Luther vigorously defended the priesthood of all believers. He opposed the Roman Church, and felt the Romanists (the Roman Catholic Church hierarchy) had skilfully built three walls around themselves "with which they protected themselves."[47]

The first wall was what the Romanists called *the spiritual estate*, which included the Pope, bishops, priests, and monks; the princes, lords, artisans, and peasants were called the *temporal estate*. In other words, it was those in the former group who were considered spiritual, while those in the other group were considered people of the world. Luther argued that all Christians were truly the spiritual estate, and there was no difference among them, save of office alone. In support, Luther quoted Paul from I Corinthians, arguing that because people in the two estates had one baptism, one gospel, and one faith, which alone made spiritual and Christian people, there was no difference between the Christians in the two estates. He went on to say,

> We are all consecrated as priests by baptism, a higher consecration in us than Pope, or bishop can give. . . Since we are all priests, no one may put himself forward, or take upon himself, without our consent and election, to do that which we have all alike power to do. . . The only real difference between laymen and priests is one of office and function, and not of estate; they are all priests, though their functions are not the same.[48]

The second wall was that the spiritual estate alone were masters of the Scriptures; "although they learn nothing from them during their entire life they assume authority, and juggle before us impudent |shameless| words, saying that the Pope cannot err in matters of faith, whether he is evil or good."[49]

The third wall was that . . . "if they are threatened with a council, they pretend that no one may call a council but the Pope. . . Now may God help us, and give us one of those trumpets that overthrew the walls of Jericho . . ."[50] Luther "insisted that the public ministry was simply a matter of practical function or vocation. It followed that it was not a higher or more religious form of life with a special standing in God's eyes."[51]

Philip Jacob Spener (1675–1705) wrote extensively on the spiritual priesthood of every Christian. His efforts were an attempt to impress on believers in his day the far-reaching implications of Luther's priesthood of all believers.[52] He advocated that the name *priest* was for all Christians; and that all Christians without distinction were spiritual priests. However, Spener did not believe that all Christians are preachers, for "to exercise the office publicly in the congregation before all and over all requires a *special call*."[53] This is the first time we learn about a special call to preaching, for in the early church it was a call to salvation.

Spener is regarded as father of pietism (religious devotion). He was born thirteen years before the end of the Thirty Years' War (CE 1618–48) between the Protestants and Catholics—when many lives were lost and suffering was inflicted on many others. Spener needs to be understood in light of that harsh historical background. Longing for a rebirth of moral earnestness in Germany, he organized small groups that met in his home for Bible reading, prayer, and discussion. As he and others met to deepen their spiritual lives, they became known as *collegia pietatis*. In 1675 Spener published a book, Pia Desideria, "in which he summoned pastors to speak the Word of God to the common man, capable and pious laymen to act as preachers, and all Christians to show love, piety, and moderation."[54]

It is important to know that during the time of Luther and Spener, many priests read sermons of great preachers such as Augustine from the pulpit; and those sermons were in Latin. Therefore, the struggle was to have a worship service with sermons, prayers, and the rest of the order of worship in the vernacular languages that people could understand.

August Hermann Francke (1663–1727), Spener's most famous student, began a pietistic study group in Leipzig in 1689. After he faced opposition at the University of Leipzig, he left for a faculty position at the newly established University of Halle. At this new university, Francke was able to include pietism in the curriculum. The faculty produced more than two hundred ministers a year for the Lutheran Church. Francke combined pietism and social work, such as establishing the famous Orphan House at Halle in 1698.

Through Spener and Francke, the Protestant Church of Germany once more possessed zealous ministers and laymen. Bible study and devotional sincerity increased; social service spread, and ministers and laymen were stirred to new seriousness. But pietism neglected intellectual pursuits. This was the pietism that influenced the Moravians, under the leadership of Count Zinzendorf, and down to John Wesley. However, Wesley came to distrust the Moravians as "still men" who would do nothing, "not even read the Bible or take communion while waiting for mystical assurance of absolute salvation."[55]

Note that the doctrine of a special call to exercise the preaching office in a congregation or local church is a strong issue in the Reformation and post-Reformation periods.[56] Also note that the missionary churches that came out of the Reformation and evangelical background in Europe emphasized a special call for the following category of leaders in the church: ordained ministers and missionaries to foreign lands. They de-emphasized the *calling of all people to God's salvation*; and consequently de-emphasized the early indigenous or African preachers, whom they preferred to call *helpers* to the missionaries, who were considered to be *called*.

Georgia Harkness, an American Methodist theologian of the mid-twentieth century, felt that as much as there was a rebirth of the priesthood of all believers during the reformation, it also had contradictions. She said, "It placed great emphasis on the pure preaching of the Word and the right administration of the sacraments as the true marks of the Church."[57] She therefore, raises the right questions when she says, "Who, but a theologically educated clergy were capable of such 'pure' preaching? And who but the ordained clergy could 'rightly' administer the sacraments?"[58]

Chapter 4

Evangelism as Mission
of the Local Church

Every local church, congregation, circuit, or parish is called into existence by God, into God's mission, which is a totality of all the Church's ministries. And in God's mission, evangelism is the heartbeat of ministry. Therefore, it is important that every local church believes it exists by divine calling and for divine purpose. And every local church needs to regard the ministry of evangelism in its community as a priority. In our church structure there is the General Conference, central conferences, annual conferences, and district conferences, and their equivalent church bodies in other denominations—all with church offices of evangelism or boards of evangelism, which is well and good. This chapter seeks to emphasize that the local church provides the most significant arena for the ministry of evangelism.

It is at the local church level where the powers of righteousness engage in battle with powers of darkness. In African communities—villages, towns, and cities—the following forces of evil are still present: fear of death, practice and fear of witchcraft, ignorance, superstition, and practice of idolatry. Some traditions still engage in horrendous and evil practices, and many other practices that hinder both human and community development. Also in these communities local churches minister to many who are hungry, sick, naked, and hopeless. In addition, due to political upheaval in some of our countries, local churches see the landless and those whose homes were set on fire by their political enemies, as well as those who may be sleeping in the bush or mountain for fear of their political enemies. Many people have lost limbs, ears, and eyes; and many others have lost their lives, leaving defenceless dependents and orphans. In the local church, prayers are directed toward God, quoting the words of the prophet Habakkuk:

How long, O LORD, must I call for help, but you do not listen? Or cry out to you, "Violence!" but you do not save? Why do you make me look at injustice? Why do you tolerate wrong? Destruction and violence are before me; there is strife, and conflict abounds. Therefore the law is paralyzed, and justice never prevails. The wicked hem in the righteous, so that justice is perverted. (Hab. 1:2–4)

Or as Amos cried out, ". . . let justice roll on like a river, righteousness like a never-failing stream!" (Amos 5:24).

According to Luke, Jesus started his battle with the Jewish establishment in a local church—a synagogue in Nazareth, where he read a passage from the scroll of the prophet Isaiah:

"The Spirit of the Lord is on me, because he has anointed me to preach good news to the poor. He has sent me to proclaim freedom for the prisoners and recovery of sight for the blind, to release the oppressed, to proclaim the year of the Lord's favor." (Luke 4:18–19)

The local church provides the most significant arena through which disciple-making occurs—that is, a place where Jesus Christ is proclaimed all the time. Christ-like life is lived and shared through word and deed. People experience the gracious love of God and are transformed as they are nurtured in the way of Christ. They are disciplined in love to help them move toward knowing the fullness Christ in their lives and their potential for his ministry. The local church provides the best opportunity for seekers coming even at night, like Nicodemus who went to ask Jesus, "How can a man be born when he is old?" (John 3:4). If we agree that the local church is the most significant arena for the ministry of evangelism to occur, then local churches must be provided with the best pastoral appointments and the best lay leadership in all positions of the local church. It also means that our resources should be mobilized to strengthen every local church as the production floor for the whole church. Africa may need to avoid the temptation to copy everything from our mother churches, who have created good general agencies of the church that may rob us of the best pastors and lay persons who could serve in a local church. Or rob us of our financial resources that could best be spent strengthening the local churches.

A few years ago, I read a book that included a chapter authored by Bishop Francis Gerald Enlsey of the Methodist Church. The bishop told a story of the risen Christ returning to heaven after his victorious mission on earth, after defeating the powers of death and sin. Upon his arrival in heaven he was warmly received by all the angels. The archangel Gabriel asked Christ a question: "Lord, now that you have come back from the earth, who will carry out your work?"

"I left Peter, John, James, and the rest of the disciples," Christ Jesus replied.

"What if they fail?" Gabriel insisted.

"I have no other plan," Jesus said as he ended the discussion.

If only every local church realized that laity are the plan of the risen Christ, regardless of where it has been planted! Local churches are planted all over villages, towns, and cities in all African nations as the plan of the risen Christ, with the Great Commission: (a) to "make disciples of all nations" (Matt. 28:19); (b) to "preach the good news to all creation" (Mark 16:15); (c) to preach "repentance and forgiveness of sins . . . in his name to all nations (Luke 24:47); and (d) to bring peace and hope to all those who live in fear in many of our African homes, villages, towns, and cities. At the same time, local churches need to be constantly conscious of the fact that as Christ was sent by the Father, he is also sending the local churches as an agent for evangelism in the villages, towns, and cities scattered on the face of the earth (John 20:19–21).

What is the mission or task of the local church in conjunction with the ministry of evangelism? What is there for the members of the church to do about evangelism in their local church? And how is the pastor to blow the trumpet that sounds a clear call for an evangelistic battle through his/her local church (1 Cor. 14:8)?

What follows in this chapter are suggestions coming from my experiences as a pastor, a listener, and a reader of the works of those who have been great pastors and teachers in the area of the ministry of evangelism—the seven great marks of an evangelistic local church.

Establishing a Worshipping Church

Offering the church's worship to God every Sunday is the first and greatest mark of an evangelistic local church. The Gospel According to Matthew shares a story about the visit of the Magi from the East to Bethlehem, who looked for Jesus so that they could worship him, for they had seen his star. Indeed, when they finally saw the child with his mother, Mary, ". . . they bowed down and worshiped him" (Matt. 2:11). Thereafter, they presented him with gifts. Similarly, when the eleven disciples met the risen Christ in Galilee at a mountain where they had been directed, almost instantly "they worshiped him" although some still had some doubts (Matt. 28:17). Some doubted as they saw him from afar, but as he drew nearer to them, they were confronted by the truth—the reality of his resurrection—as death had stripped him of those bonds of time and space that tie all men and women to this earth.[59] Yes, he was a free person. And immediately, the eleven were moved to worship him.

Often, worshippers have expectations as they prepare to attend a Sunday worship service. Some of these expectations are noble, and others ignoble. Some expectations are captured and met in the Order of Sunday Worship, as we will see later. The pastor needs always to prepare for each part of the Order of Sunday Worship because each part conveys the saving grace as people come together to offer their worship to God.

I recall my first worship service as pastor of Grace United Methodist Church in Springfield, Illinois, in July 1970. It was a Holy Communion service. After delivering the message, I began receiving people at the altar kneeling rail. As the congregation sang, I found tears streaming down my cheeks. Surprisingly, as the communicants came forward, I discovered I was sharing the same emotional response with the congregation. We all testified it was a moving worship service.

Some expectations for Sunday worship may not be captured in the Order of Worship. I shall try to relate those expectations as we look at a few of the items in the Order of Worship of The United Methodist Church that enhance an evangelistic atmosphere in worship.

First, *call to worship*: A call to worship is an occasion to alert and simultaneously invite the congregation to begin offering their worship to God. In Zimbabwe, among the Manyika of the Shona people, when a gathering realizes the presence of their chief, or anyone of the chieftainship family, someone will announce, *"Ngatikwidze mawoko kuna Mambo or Ishe"* (Let us clap our hands as a way to recognise the chief). At the announcement all other conversations stop. Words of greeting and praise are uttered simultaneously with men clapping hands first, to be followed by the women, who clap in their own way and ululate at the same time. Recognizing members of chieftainship by a gathering is a sign that whatever business is to be discussed or carried out has already begun; it also implies that all have turned their minds away from everything else and are ready to hear from the chief.

Likewise, a call to worship in church summons the people to concentrate on worshipping God—including those who still have wondering and doubtful minds. What an opportunity for the pastor or liturgist to stand and request the congregation to rise for the call to worship, announcing: "I was glad when they said unto me, Let us go into the house of the LORD" (Ps. 122:1, KJV).

33

Or, "Come to me, all you who are weary and burdened, and I will give you rest. Take my yoke upon you and learn from me, for I am gentle and humble in heart, and you will find rest for your souls. For my yoke is easy and my burden is light" (Matt. 11:28–30).

Using either of the above texts as a call to worship will meet someone's need, and probably trigger a few amens. There are many biblical texts suitable for a call to worship, and there are many ways of planning calls to worship. The point is that congregations should plan the call to worship to meet expectations of people and announce the call to worship in a lively way.

Second, the *first congregational hymn*: A call to worship needs to be followed by a powerful congregational hymn such as "M'*tsene*, M'*tsvene*, M'*svene*" (Holy, Holy, Holy). As much as I love choir singing, asking the congregation to sit while the choir to sings first is like quenching the Spirit (1 Thess. 5:19). Immediately after a call to worship the congregation should burst forth with a great hymn of praise and thanksgiving. This is the time when God must hear the voices of all the children who gather to offer their worship to God. That first hymn may determine for some visitors whether they want to come back to that local church. The church should sing with joy and hope for something greater that is to come. The church should show its joy that *now* they are in the house of the Lord.

Third, *the affirmation of faith*: The singing of a great opening hymn is often followed by the affirmation of faith, like the Apostles' Creed: "I believe in God the Father Almighty, maker of heaven and earth. And in Jesus Christ, his only Son our Lord. I believe in the Holy Spirit, the holy catholic Church, the communion of saints."

The affirmation is a proclamation of the gospel. I often wish the congregation would rehearse the recitation of this affirmation together from time to time so that when the congregation stands to declare the affirmation in a Sunday worship it demonstrates that we really believe it from our hearts. An evangelistic church would declare it with joy, because it is proclaiming the gospel to all non-believers.

Fourth, *the pastoral prayer*: This prayer is the monopoly of the pastor for he/she alone carries the burden of the flock—members and the people of the community. The prayer is characterized by the following elements: (a) adoration—recognition of God as God; (b) invocation—calling upon God to assist those gathered in their worship (Rom. 8:26); (c) confession—repentance in order to be renewed; (d) thanksgiving—response to the gospel of God's grace; (e) supplication—prayer for our own needs; (f) Intercession—prayer to God for other people's needs (the sick, the bereaved, the troubled are lifted in prayer). People often feel their burdens rolled away when they hear the pastor praying for problems they struggle with; (g) illumination—prayer that precedes preaching; (h) oblation—prayer as a corporate act. In the pastoral prayer, avoid singular pronouns—"I pray. . ." A believer never prays alone. Remember when Elijah said to God, "'I am the only one left, and now they are trying to kill me too' . . . The Lord said to him, 'Go back the way you came . . . I reserved seven thousand in Israel—all whose knees have not bowed down to Baal and all whose mouths have not kissed him'" (1 Kings 19:10–18). It is good for each member of a local church to know that when he/she prays for something in their church or community there may be another ten or twenty members who are praying to God for the same issue. Prayer is corporate. Use the plural pronouns "we" or "us," for many are always praying, often at the same time, though we may be kilometres apart. Such understanding of prayer binds the church together, and is a mark of an evangelistic church.

Fifth, *choir singing*: The role of the choir is to lead the whole congregation in worship, not to stage a concert that reduces the congregation to spectators. The choir has its place in the order of worship and a good choir can be a blessing toward achieving goals of evangelism. When I was pastor of Grace United Methodist Church, the evangelistic work achieved there was built on the work of the youth choir and youth ministry. When I became Vice Chancellor of Africa University, one of the earliest recruits was Patrick Matsikinyiri, who established the University Choir that has become reputable worldwide. A vibrant local church will need witnessing choir(s), including *Vabvuwi*, *Rukwadzano*, and youth choirs. Good singing in a local church by the choir draws many to the church, and God can speak to many though such a ministry of music.

Sixth, *Bible reading*: It is important to read the Bible in the early stage of the Order of Service. Reading a text from the Old Testament and another from the New Testament is a good practice. Others may read one passage from the Old Testament, another from the Letters, and the last from the Gospels. Maintaining that order is following a good old tradition. Bible readers should be told well in advance so that they have time to rehearse their reading, for good reading amounts to proclamation itself.

Seventh, *announcements*: Church announcements should not take too much time. Some people take announcements as their time to show and prove who they are. As a result they end up taking a long time. One solution, for those who can afford it, is to print the Order of Worship and include announcements for members to read themselves.

Eighth, *preaching*: Sunday preaching is central to Sunday worship. Everything in the worship order builds up to the time when the Word is proclaimed; and whatever comes later in the order of worship must not distort the Word preached. Good preaching focuses on the gospel—preaching Christ contextually, or in relation to the situation of the people. Avoid using the pulpit as a place to attack other people or one's enemies. Often, long sermons are a result of an unprepared preacher. Good preaching delivers the message of the day, urgently and passionately, after which the preacher stops.

One cannot prescribe a worship pattern for all local churches, but if each one of the above parts of worship is done timely, especially in towns and cities, the Sunday morning service will attract a significant number of people. Gone are the days when a preacher would stand in the pulpit and say, "In Africa the sun never sets." It does set. Or, "In Africa we do not have to worry about time." People do worry about time nowadays, especially when there is a football game taking place that afternoon. Neither should we view those who go for soccer on Sunday as less spiritual than the so-called committed ones.

Establishing an Evangelistic Preaching Church

For a local church to build an effective evangelistic preaching ministry, the following factors need close attention.

First, *the pulpit must lift up Christ.* "Just as Moses lifted up the snake in the desert, so the Son of Man must be lifted up, that everyone who believes in him may have eternal life" (John 3:14–15). James Stewart, a great Scottish preacher and homilitician of the 1940s, describes a conversation of two preachers who had not seen each other for a long time. One of the two preachers reported, "Whatever we started off with in our conversations, we soon made across the country, somehow to Jesus of Nazareth, to His death, and His resurrection, and His indwelling. . ."[60] So it is with an evangelistic preaching local church. Whether it is the pastor or lay preacher, no matter where one may start off in a sermon, ultimately Christ must be lifted up in such away that the listeners may decide for themselves to follow him or not.

Today, African urban churches are bombarded by visitors who attend our church services on a Sunday for the first time. One Sunday, my wife and I were invited to participate in a worship service at St. John's United Methodist Church in Mutare, Zimbabwe. I was amazed to see the number of young people and young couples who attended the service. At the end of the service I asked the pastor if he knew all those young people who came. He answered that he knew those who were members of St. John's, but a number of them were visitors. Young people and young couples in our African cities have an interest in attending Sunday church services, especially when services are conducted in the morning.

What an opportunity that the local church in Africa has today to proclaim the gospel of Jesus Christ. In the Methodist tradition, evangelistic preaching is defined as the proclamation that offers Christ to the people. "Offer them Christ," John Wesley exhorted the young preacher, Francis Asbury, as he was set to sail for America in 1771. God has already offered his Son to the world, so that whoever believes in him has eternal life; likewise, the local church in any community is to lift up and offer Christ to the people.

Second, *proclaim the promises of God in the Bible*. In order for a local church to work toward the goal of establishing an evangelistic preaching church, its preachers need to be familiar with the promises of God in the Bible. Our preachers, be they clergy or laity, must learn to unpack these biblical promises that are so pregnant with what God can do for the people. Listen to a few of the promises in the scriptures: (a) "What is that in your hand?" (Exod. 4:2). That means Almighty God has endowed a gift or a talent in the hand of each person and that gift needs to be discovered and used. (b) "For I know the plans I have for you . . . plans to prosper you and not to harm you, plans to give you hope and a future" (Jer. 29:11). People long to hear the message of hope from the pulpit. (c) "Ask and it will be given to you; seek and you will find; knock and the door will be opened to you" (Matt.7:7). We African people and our governments have become beggars, even though we have the richest continent on earth in natural and mineral resources, because we do not know what to ask for, what to seek, and on which doors to knock. (d) "Come to me, all you who are weary and burdened, and I will give you rest" (Matt. 11:28). Think of the people burdened with problems inflicted upon them by others or by their social and economic circumstances. What a promise it is to exchange one's heavy burden for a lighter one. (e) "Here I am! I stand at the door and knock. If anyone hears my voice and opens the door, I will come in and eat with him, and he with me" (Rev. 3:20). What a privilege to have lunch at the chief's place!

Chances are that when each of these promises is expounded through an evangelistic message they will speak to someone in the congregation. This is only part of an inexhaustible range of divine promises that invite exposition—divine promises filled with the gracious evangelistic message of God through his Son.

Third, *emphasize doctrinal preaching.* Merrill Abbey, Professor of Preaching at Garrett Theological Seminary in the 1960s and 1970s and my mentor in graduate studies in preaching, wrote, "The real power of pulpit evangelism—to note but one further area—rests on a doctrinal substructure. Sin, grace, atonement, repentance and forgiveness, regeneration: these are the potent |mighty| themes of the evangelist."[61] Of course one has to remember:

> Christian doctrine is not a system, but a life; and Christian doctrine is the interpretation of a life . . . Christian doctrines are an attempt to express in words of formal statement the nature of God and Man and the World, and the relations between them, as revealed in the person and life of Jesus.[62]

Christianity has one doctrine—knowing God through Jesus Christ and the illumination of the Holy Spirit. Blessed is a pastor who thrives in doctrinal preaching—for he/she is not struggling with a system of ideas, but with the life of Jesus Christ and how he reveals and teaches humankind on such issues. He teaches us about God the Father, his love, mercy, forgiveness, and justice. All these and many others are doctrines that can be expounded from the pulpit in a local church. We have people in our communities or even in our local churches who have never known what it means to be loved and to love; or what it means to receive mercy and to be merciful to someone; or to be forgiven and to forgive another person; or to experience justice and to render justice even to their own family; and to live a life of hope for a better day or future. Several doctrinal substructures are full of the gospel of grace that needs to be proclaimed Sunday after Sunday from the pulpit of the local church. A local church that is taught and feeds on the living doctrine through proclamation by vibrant preachers will truly discover what it means to build an effective evangelistic preaching ministry in its community.

Fourth, *the pastor's and preacher's confidence in themselves as evangelists.* If a pastor or a local preacher is going to preach evangelistically he/she needs to believe he/she is an evangelist. What one thinks of oneself is important. When Paul made the charge to Timothy to ". . . do the work of an evangelist. . ." (2 Tim. 4:5), Paul was not asking Timothy to be what he was not, or could not do. Paul knew Timothy as a capable pastor—one who held his head high in all pastoral situations, one who had endured hardships, and was strong enough to discharge all pastoral duties, including the one important task—the work of an evangelist.

Some Christians, including some pastors, perceive only of certain pastors and local preachers as evangelists, and they discredit themselves as merely pastors who could not be an evangelist. So, when they plan for a revival they are always looking for other persons beyond themselves. Someone has said, "Your life is what you believe";[63] or your ministry is what you believe it to be. Actually, the Bible says, "For as he thinketh in his heart, so is he" (Prov. 23:7, KJV). If a pastor believes God has called him/her to be a pastor-evangelist, he/she becomes one; and if a lay person believes he/she has been called to do the work of an evangelist, he/she becomes an evangelist.

A number of years ago, I conducted a "Two by Two Lay Visitation Evangelism" workshop in a local church in Mutare, Zimbabwe. The time came when we the congregation presented names of persons to visit. After a name was brought forward, the leader asked, "We want two people to visit Mr. Tume (not his real name); any volunteers?"

One woman rose to her feet and offered, "I am Mrs. Tume. Now that I have been taught how to share the gospel, even to family members, I am willing to go and talk to him about Christ; and I do not need another person to accompany me." This was the first case of its kind in the workshops that we held that a spouse offered to be the only visitor, and to go back to her own home and offer Christ to a spouse. This is the kind of confidence we need to cultivate—as pastors, local preachers, and members of the local church—that we are evangelists and we can introduce another person, even a member of our family, to Christ.

Further, every preacher, clergyperson, or layperson, needs to have confidence in the message that we preach. Often it is not a good sermon that gets to people; it is God's message conveyed through the sermon. At times, that message gets to people in spite of the sermon. The Lord spoke through the Prophet Isaiah:

> As the rain and the snow come down from heaven, and do not return to it without watering the earth and making it bud and flourish, so that it yields seed for the sower and bread for the eater, so is my word that goes out from my mouth: it will not return to me empty, but will accomplish what I desire and achieve the purpose for which I sent it. (Isa. 55:10–11)

A man was stealing green maize from his neighbour's garden. He had his son with him, whom he instructed to climb on the garden fence to watch if anyone was coming to the garden. After the man had his bag filled with stolen maize and he was ready to leave, the child called to his father—a call that made his father panic.

"What is it? Did you see someone?" the dad asked.

"No, Dad! You asked me to watch if anyone would come from the north or south, east or west, but how about from heavenward?"

Hearing those words, the father emptied his bag of stolen maize, and he and his son left immediately.

The son had delivered the message from heavenward—a message that changed the father. Not only do we need to have confidence in ourselves as the change agents of God in our communities, we also need to have confidence in the message that we preach as a divine message to God's people.

Fifth, *the altar call.* In his discussion of biblical interpretation and evangelistic preaching, William Sangster, a great English Methodist preacher of the 1950s, wrote, "Where the evangelical appeal is rarely or never sounded, an awful incompleteness hangs over the whole work."[64] A local church that desires an effective evangelistic preaching ministry needs for its pastor(s) and local preachers to be comfortable with extending an altar call, without abusing it, at the end of the evangelistic message. The biblical background and theological rationale for the practice of an altar call is this: "The altar-call is an invitation to Christian discipleship."[65] It is an appeal to make a public commitment to Christ by individuals who have not done so. It is an encouragement to persons who might want to make a commitment or to start their lives over—call it a re-dedication or another beginning. Often people want to express their response to the gospel after the Word has been proclaimed. As John the Baptist preached around the Jordan, the crowd, tax collectors, and some soldiers asked him, "What should we do then?" (Luke 3:10). Similarly, after Peter had preached on the day of Pentecost, the people who heard the message asked Peter and the other apostles, "Brothers, what shall we do?" (Acts 2:37). Therefore, the pastor or local preacher must learn to extend an altar call at the end of his or her message to provide a time for the people to respond.

The biblical or historical and theological bases for the significance of extending an altar call is traced back to the Old Testament, where we understand the altar as "a place of sacrifice near which animals were slaughtered and on which oblations of corn, wine, and incense were burnt and offered, in the open air."[66] This altar was furnished with a horn at each of its four corners (Exod. 27:2). The horns symbolised power (Deut. 33:17; Num. 23:22; Ps. 18:2). Before the "centralisation of worship at the Jerusalem Temple and the consequent provision of cities of refuge (Deut. 19:1–13), altars provided sanctuary for fugitives suspected of murder, who 'took hold of the horns at the altar' and were safe pending their trial (cf. 1 Kings 2:28),"[67] (1 Kings 1:50). Altars were imbued not just with power but also with holiness, and became a place where people found salvation or refuge.[68]

In the New Testament Jesus is understood as God's sacrifice of atonement. By faith in Jesus' blood (Rom. 3:25) shed on the altar, humankind is enabled to see God once more. Or through the life, ministry, death, resurrection, the coming of the promise of the Holy Spirit, and exaltation to the right hand of God of Jesus, God is in Christ reconciling the world to himself (2 Cor. 5:19).

When a pastor or a local preacher extends an altar call, he or she is pointing to One greater than himself or herself. The altar symbolizes a greater Presence than that of the preacher in front of the congregation. It means inviting people to become disciples of Christ or to embark on a life of Christian discipleship. As one extends the invitation for people to come to the altar, likewise, the preacher should leave the pulpit and come down to meet such persons who respond at the communion rail. However, the effectiveness of an altar call depends on the clarity with which it is extended. "If the trumpet does not sound a clear call, who will get ready for battle?" Paul said (1 Cor. 14:8).

There is a tradition where the pastor calls people to come and kneel at the altar before he or she has preached. This is so they may dedicate themselves to God, or pray or unburden themselves before God of any concerns they may have. There are church members who may also feel that wherever they kneel to pray in spirit and truth is an altar. The pastor should never force participation at the altar, because God's altar of grace should not be viewed only as geographical, but also as spiritual. There is always unspeakable joy to the shepherd in seeing the sheep coming into the fold, responding to the inward call of the great Shepherd—coming for both reconciliation and total healing. That is the experience and joy the local church that is striving to establish an effective evangelistic preaching ministry in its community may experience Sunday after Sunday.

Establishing a Bible-Studying Church

Establishing a Bible-studying church is the third and great mark of an evangelistic local church. In November 2010, American management expert Stephen Covey spoke in Harare on "The Art of Leadership and Its Impact on Organizational Success." In his speech he pointed out that companies and institutions need to realize that the world is moving from an Industrial Age to a Knowledge Worker Age, where we have to recognize that every one of us is born with magnificent gifts, talents, capacities, privileges, intelligences, and opportunities with infinite potentials. He also advocated for high trust leadership where control is superseded by empowerment, because most organizations have employees with immense talent that is waiting to be unlocked.[69]

About 55 and 57 CE, Paul wrote about the early Church as one body—the body of Christ—composed of people with diverse spiritual gifts (1 Cor. 12:1–13) and different gifts (Rom. 12:1–8) respectively. Those spiritual gifts are often recognized when people search for purposeful meaning in their life and the world. Conversion of one's life to Christ often provides that fulfilment and a new destiny in life. Reading or studying the Bible often provides that turning point for individual Christians such as Augustine, who suffered from self disgust because of his inability to control his sexual desires. At the height of his struggle he fled from his friends and went into a garden where he felt he heard the voice of a child commanding him to "take and read." Having a copy of Paul's letter to the Romans, his eyes fell on the passage in the thirteenth chapter that included the following:

> Let us behave decently, as in the daytime, not in orgies
> |secret or wild rites| and drunkenness, not in sexual
> immorality and debauchery, not in dissension and jeal-
> ousy. Rather, clothe yourselves with the Lord Jesus Christ,
> and do not think about how to gratify the desires of the
> sinful nature. (Rom. 13:13–14).

When Augustine obeyed the voice of a child and picked up Paul's letter to the Romans and read it, the passage transformed his whole life and channelled his great intellectual powers into his work as Bishop of Hippo and a great leader of the Christian Church.

The major purpose in efforts to read and study the Bible is religious,[70] and one of the great achievements of Bible societies has been to make the Bible available in the vernacular languages of as many peoples on earth as possible. In our African local churches there are persons who have no access to any other book than the Bible. Such persons read their Bible almost daily, but they do not always understand what they read. They are like the Ethiopian eunuch who read the scriptures on his chariot as he travelled back to his country. Philip asked him, "Do you understand what you are reading?" His reply was, "How can I, unless someone explains it to me?" (Acts 8:30–31). This episode presents the challenge to pastors. The Bible needs explanation, and there is no better teacher in our parishes, circuits, or local churches than pastors who have been appointed there.

In relation to church life, our local churches are packed with individual members endowed with gifts or talents that the church as an institution does not use properly, primarily because of the church's emphasis on control instead of empowerment. Bible study empowers the laity; it enables them to realize what they can do instead of simply hearing the interpretation of the scriptures by the clergy. There is need for the church to recognize the various gifts and talents that people have and to empower them so that they achieve their infinite potential in fulfilling the mission of the church in the community and the larger society. For that to happen, every local church needs to have a viable Bible-study programme as part of its mission for evangelism. Bible study unlocks untold talents and gifts that the local church may possess. Here are some guidelines for local churches as they develop Bible-study programmes.

First, *the pastor and Bible study*. The pastor should take the lead in studying the Bible, and in leading a Bible-study group or groups at the church. As Dwight Stevenson says to pastors and preachers, "Before you can preach from the Bible you should settle the question of the relationship of scripture to the Word of God. To be fuzzy on this point is to confuse the preaching ministry from start to finish."[71] The position taken by the great reformers John Calvin and Martin Luther and others was that: (a) Jesus Christ is the Word of God; (b) the Bible is the Word of God (or written Word) in a secondary or derivative sense because it is about Christ; and, (c) preaching is the Word of God, or spoken word of God because it is from the Bible. Usually, what the pastor or preacher believes about the Bible is what his/her congregation is going to believe. A pastor leaves a lasting impression on listeners about what he/she believes about the Bible. However, our congregations today include members who have taken some courses in religion, or have developed critical minds about what the Bible says. The pastor needs to continue studying his Bible for his/her own sake, and for purposes of teaching and preaching.

Second, *the pastor as the trainer of the laity*. The pastor should train the laity who may be interested in leading Bible study groups either at the church or class meetings or and in the sections. Groups should not be forced on people, but there are always several people in every local church who want to study the Bible. Often their problem is finding someone to teach them. Although *class meetings* in the Methodist Societies in England originated as a way of raising funds for the rebuilding of a Society New Room in Bristol, eventually they developed into a unit of Society membership (12 members), and the training ground of lay leaders, who became strong instruments of evangelism and Christian education.[72] The introduction and training of the laity in preaching, teaching, and participating in the leadership of propagating the gospel was the genius of the Methodist Revival of the eighteenth century.

Many of our congregations have members who belong to professions such as teaching, agriculture, technology, and civil service. These persons are always a blessing to the church. Some of these people could be considered to lead Bible study groups of members, for the pastor may not be able to carry out all the Bible teaching alone. Indeed, there are those whose gift of teaching is already known by their local church, and it should be utilized. However, it is the pastor, who reads and continues studying his Bible, who will be a good example in guiding his/her church in Bible study.

Third, *the venue for Bible study.* Bible-study groups can meet at the church, in the homes of church members, or anywhere else it is convenient. The Bible-study group led by the pastor will most likely meet in the church building.

Fourth, *special groups where Bible study could be organized.* Bible study can also be emphasized in confirmation or initiation classes. It can also be held in church groups such as the Women's Organization, Men's Organization, and the youth group. Additionally, Bible study can be integrated into church choir retreats and other church events.

Fifth, *the literacy class.* If a pastor is appointed to a parish or circuit where illiteracy is high among adult members of the church, there is an opportunity to introduce a literacy class. I have discovered that most of the members of the church who are illiterate have a desire to read the Bible and sing from the hymn book for themselves. I also observed that the desire to read the Bible and to sing from the hymnal motivated these people to attend literacy classes. When I introduced a literacy class in a rural circuit where I served, I was amazed by people who registered as students and consistently attended class until they were able to read the Bible for themselves.

Sixth, *the benefits of Bible study in a local church.* There are many benefits to Bible study: (a) Bible study brings about the *spirit of renewal* in the local church (2 Kings 22:8ff; Acts 8:26-40). (b) Bible Study reinforces *the spirit of confidence in reading our Bibles.* Many church members read the Bible alone at home and live with unanswered questions in their efforts to study the Bible. (c) An effective Bible-study programme unlocks gifts, talents, capacities, and opportunities for people so that they grow toward the realization of their potential. (d) The Bible is not just about spiritual things; it also about talents (Matt. 25:14–30), gifts (1 Cor. 12: 4–11), and health care and healing (Mark 1:30; 2:1–5; Acts 3:1–10; 1 Tim. 5:23). (e) Through Bible study, people can be transformed intellectually, socially, and spiritually as they are inspired and challenged "to know and experience God through Jesus Christ, claim and live God's promises, and grow and serve as Christian disciples."[73]

Finally, *Bible study must be done evangelistically.* Billy Graham shared a story of a young woman who had heard of an interesting book. She went to a bookshop and bought the book. She started reading, yet hardly finished the introduction when she put it away. Later on she heard other people praising the same book. She went back home, forced herself to read only to the end of the first chapter, and put it away again. It happened she went on a summer holiday where she met a young, handsome man. The two fell in love, only for her to realise that the young man was the author of the book she could hardly read. After she got home from her holiday, she read the whole book within a short time. Why? She now was in love with the author of the book. When we love God with all our heart, soul, mind, and strength, Bible reading and study become a delight upon which we meditate day and night (Ps.1:2).

Establishing a Praying Church

A praying church is the fourth great mark of an evangelistic local church. The Church in Africa has been known as a praying church. As a student of theology, I attended a workshop conducted by two renowned

48

professors, one of whom was George Buttrick. There I heard a profound definition of prayer: "Prayer is conversation with God." As I thought on it, my mind was taken to Nehemiah who while in exile had a visit from his brother and other men who had just come from land of Judah. After hearing about the situation at home—the trouble and disgrace his people suffered and how the walls of Jerusalem had been broken down and its gates burned—Nehemiah sat down and wept. In his tears, Nehemiah turned to God and prayed, or had a conversation with God in prayer (Neh. 1:4–11). There are times we are prompted by the Holy Spirit to pray, and in that prayer the Spirit helps us, for we might not even know what to say to God (Rom. 8:26). At the same time, we have to learn to pray always or continually (1 Thess. 5:17; Eph. 6:18). Prayer is more an attitude than it is the words we utter. Prayer is turning our whole mind and spirit to God in the power of the Holy Spirit—delighting and meditating in his Word day and night (Ps. 1:2).

We may not always have an opportunity to kneel and pray; at times we may have to pray as we walk, drive, or work. I have heard that some people sing as they work in their fields, and that singing is prayer to God, a conversation with God. We do not have to wait until we get to a church building in order to pray; Jesus taught his disciples, ". . . go into your room, close the door and pray to your Father, who is unseen. Then your Father, who sees what is done in secret, will reward you" (Matt. 6:6). He taught his disciples how to pray always:

> Praise your Father's name all the time;
>   Ask for his kingdom to come on earth,
>   and especially in your situation,
>   and for His will to be done;
>   Ask for the daily food and;
>   any other needs,
>   Ask for forgiveness for our moral debts,
>   and also for the spirit and capacity to forgive others;

Thank the Father for not leading us into temptation, but ask to be delivered from evil—such as, wrongdoing, illness, and witchcraft, or especially the fear of witchcraft.

A Christian who regards himself/herself as a true child of God can have a conversation with God, our Father, on all these things—and God hears and responds to our requests; only he does not always respond the way we expect or want, as he said through the Prophet Isaiah:

"For my thoughts are not your thoughts, neither are your ways my ways. . . As the heavens are higher than the earth, so are my ways higher than your ways and my thoughts than your thoughts." (Isa. 55:8–9)

In our asking him, we are not telling him what to do about our situation. No, we never tell God what to do, just as we do not tell our earthly fathers what to do. Hence his response to Paul, who had described his agonizing situation as "a thorn in my flesh, a messenger of Satan." God answered, "My grace is sufficient for you, for my power is made perfect in weakness" (2 Cor. 12:9). Paul presented a request to God in prayer, and God responded to Paul in an attitude of prayer. Yes, prayer is conversation with God.

People want to talk to God about many things. Often, they include the problems they experience in life. One Sunday morning I drove to my village home. Before I got there, about 8 a.m., I saw a young woman trotting, going the same direction I was going. I stopped my car and gave her a lift.

"Where are you going so early in the morning?" I asked.

"I am going to church," she answered.

"What time does your church service begin?" I asked.

"It starts at 10 a.m.. However, I want to get there early because at about 9 a.m. there is a special prayer session for those who have problems. And I do not want to miss that prayer session." She was longing for that moment, when together with other members of her church she would have a conversation with God. As we arrived at her church, I commended her for taking her burdens to God, for Jesus specifically invited those who were weary and burdened to come to him so that he could give them rest (Matt. 11:28).

In communities wherever our local churches are, many people experience devastating powers of evil in their lives. There are married couples who want children but are childless; there are couples who since they got married have experienced constant arguments and fighting—some leading to death. Due to political upheaval in some countries, there are men and women who are at home during the day, and at night they sleep in the mountains or in the forest; there are many of them whose houses and all their household belongings have been burned to ashes, so they are left with nothing. There are persons in the communities where our local churches exist who are poverty-stricken—they cannot afford more than one meal a day, and others go for days without a single meal. Some families are so poor that they can't even afford the minimal fees for a wife to deliver her baby in a clinic or hospital. Many cannot afford medical treatment when they are ill.

The victims of so many social forces—I call them evil powers—must be wondering if our local churches cannot bring deliverance to their lives. One day I listened with interest and delight as my nephew shared with me the great work that was being done in their circuit by one of our graduates from Africa University, Faculty of Theology. My nephew had just come from a visit that was part of a programme introduced by the new pastor. Some men and women of their congregation had been assigned to visit elderly persons—members of the church who can no longer afford to come because of old age, and other elderly persons in the community. The purpose of the visit was to pray with them, and to see how the congregation could continue ministering to them. That was a great programme.

A local church that plans to reach out to people in its community will need to develop a prayer ministry in the congregation and in the homes of people in the community. Here are some hints for a local church that wishes to develop into a praying church:

First, *learn from Jesus.* A local church that wants to be a praying church will have to learn from Jesus, who truly regarded "prayer as conversation with God."[74] It is important to study together (a) What Jesus taught about prayer (Matt. 6:5-13), and the parable of the Pharisee and the Tax Collector (Luke 18:9–14); (b) How Jesus lived an exemplary life of prayer: "While it was still dark, Jesus got up, left the house and went off to a solitary place, where he prayed" (Mark 1:35); Jesus praying in a solitary place, before calling the first disciples (Luke 4:42–5:11); Jesus in Gethsemane (Mark 14:35; Matt. 26:39; Luke 22:41).

Second, *prayer is a corporate ministry.* No one ever prays alone. Elijah learned that lesson when he thought he was the only one left (1Kings 19:14), only to learn that there were *"seven thousand in Israel*—all whose knees have not bowed down to Baal and all whose mouths have not kissed him" (1 Kings 19:18). Even when you kneel down as an individual, you are not alone in prayer. Many Christians in a family pray for each other; Christians in a local church pray for their fellow members; Christians in a nation pray for their leaders; and Christians pray for those falsely accused of things they never did. If we think of prayer that way, we begin to realize that prayer is a great force. Indeed, prayer is a corporate ministry for Christians—we intercede for others, even those we do not know, who need our prayer. Therefore, organize your congregation for a prayer ministry—prayer groups, prayer partners, prayer retreats, twenty-four-hour prayer ministries, prayer hot lines, prayer requests, prayer cards, and healing prayer services.

Third, *prayer cells*. William Sangster proposes four types of prayer cells that can be established in a local church: (a) Family Prayer Cell—where families are encouraged to engage in regular prayers at their own convenient time. Children often learn to pray during family prayers. Even when children are no longer at home, they know that Dad and Mum are at home praying for each one of them by name. It is also in such family prayers that children learn to pray for one another, and for their parents also. Family prayers are the most appropriate arena for prayer training. My father and mother were persons of prayer, and they led us in prayer every evening after supper. (b) Business Prayer Cell—where business groups of men or women meet at a convenient time, either for breakfast (in urban areas) or for a cup of tea in homes (especially for women) focusing on prayer. (c) Neighbourhood Prayer Cell—where prayer groups meet, not only in the homes of believers, but also in the homes of seekers who may extend an invitation for such prayers in their homes. (d) Church Prayer Cell—where local church members may pray for a special event, such as praying for rain, for an upcoming revival meeting, for the young people of the community, or for peace during an upcoming election.[75]

There are moments in life when we are unable to talk to someone else about our problems, and when other people no longer know what to say to us. Some years ago, I read a story in a magazine of a man who was dying of cancer. The man was in pain, and the family had done everything possible to help relieve him of the pain. As he groaned in agony, a neighbour arrived and in an attempt to comfort him he uttered the usual statement in that rural village:

"Mukute [not his real name], die like a man."

The replay came swiftly, "How does a man die?"

The neighbour could not answer the dying man's question. I suppose he immediately learned the lesson that at times it is better to be silent when faced by a situation you do not understand. "Die like a man?" Yes, "'Father, into your hands I commit my spirit.' When he had said this, he breathed his last" (Luke 23:46). Jesus died like a man; he died in a conversation of prayer with his Father.

Establishing a Fellowship (*Koinonia*) Church

Establishing a fellowship (koinonia) church is the fifth great mark of an evangelistic local church. The local church can be described best as the *koinonia*—the fellowship or a communion, meaning a sharing of possessions in common. The early church in Jerusalem "devoted themselves to the apostles' teaching and to the fellowship" (Acts 2:42). Central to their fellowship or to what they shared together was "breaking of bread" (Acts 2:42), which they did every day "in their homes and ate together with glad and sincere hearts" (Acts 2:46), without any fear of *muroyi* (a witch).

In his first letter to the church in Corinth (1 Cor. 11:17ff), Paul writes about the early church fellowship, which at that time was a divided fellowship. His writing reveals to us the two meals that took place in the church as a fellowship: (a) There was the ordinary meal or supper, to which members of the church brought food from their homes. Those who had more food were encouraged to bring more, not just for themselves, but for the sake of the poor also; and everyone was to wait for others in order to share their resources, without anyone getting drunk with wine, or leaving for home hungry. (b) There was the Lord's Supper, where again everyone was to participate. As Paul emphasized to the Corinthian church, "Is not the cup of thanksgiving for which we give thanks a participation in the blood of Christ? And is not the bread that we break a participation in the body of Christ? Because there is one loaf, we, who are many, are one body, for we all partake of the one loaf" (1 Cor. 10:16–17).

Time and again, the local church as a fellowship is supposed to come together, in spite of divisions that may occur. The church as a fellowship gains more by promoting unity than when it becomes an agent of disunity. In Africa there are communities where both property and human beings are burned because of political and religious divisions. As a new community of fellowship, the church in Africa needs to be an example of an inclusive community for a broken and divided Africa. Some examples of this are as following:

First, *testimonies as a way of fellowship.* On the second day of the first session of the East Central Africa Mission Conference, 17 November 1901, Bishop Hartzell led the "Love-feast" service at St. Andrew's Methodist Episcopal Church, Mutare, Southern Rhodesia, where participants shared testimonies. That practice, started over a hundred years ago in Zimbabwe, has stayed with us to this day. Testimonies are an enriching celebration of Christian fellowship in the life The United Methodist Church in Zimbabwe. Terence Ranger, who for years has worked on the history of Zimbabwe, and lately is professor of race relations and chair of the African Studies Committee at the University of Oxford, wrote this about African United Methodist testimonies:

African Christian testimonies—made use of and interpreted in all these ways—constituted a major genre of both official and popular Methodism in eastern Zimbabwe and Mozambique. Nothing similar survives for eastern Zimbabwean Catholicism and Anglicanism. AMEC |American Methodist Episcopal Church| missionaries not only had a particular interest in testimonies, they also had a particular interest in sermons.[76]

Second, *hymn singing.* How wonderful it would be for local churches to meet for hymn singing once every month or even more often than that. We could enjoy singing familiar hymns and learn to sing some hymns better than we do, and also learn to sing new hymns and ecumenical songs or choruses. I learned to sing Christmas carols and other hymns while at Goromonzi High School, because the student body met every Friday for about forty-five minutes to rehearse the hymns to be sung in the following Sunday worship, and to learn new hymns. It was great fellowship time. In the Zimbabwe Episcopal Area singing competitions are held for church choirs, and at times for other church groups. This is all good and part of promoting fellowship within the church.

Third, *fellowship and food*. I often think about a fellowship practice that I experienced as I grew up in Sherukuru United Methodist Church. As Christmas approached, the church people bought an ox or cow from someone in the community. Since they did not have money to pay for the beast, they would work for whoever offered the animal. They worked in the field, moulded breaks, or did whatever was needed by the owner of the beast. The animal was slaughtered, and the whole beast was cooked. Everybody came together for fellowship at the church, including many visitors from the community. People ate together during the day, and in the evening, in spite of poor lighting, they gathered in the church building where various groups made presentations such as singing songs, and children recited poems or presented dramas. Both adults and children participated in the event. That was fellowship—the local church as *koinonia*.

Thank God there are some churches that still organize Christmas parties, but often it is primarily for themselves and their families. The question is: In what ways can we reach out to the community so that we witness to Christ through the church as a fellowship?

Establishing a Community-Caring Church

A community-caring church is the sixth great mark of an evangelistic local church. Often Jesus presented his message through parables—short, simple stories that taught moral, religious, or life-situation lessons. A local church that is going to be a community-caring church will have to take its biblical and theological cue from the following two parables that Jesus shared with his disciples. (a) In the first parable, Jesus talked about a man travelling from Jerusalem to Jericho who fell into the hands of robbers. After being stripped of his clothes and beaten, the man was left almost dead. A priest and Levite who saw the helpless man on the road gave no assistance. A Samaritan who also saw him attended to the victim by giving him first aid, taking him to an inn, and paying to the innkeeper two silver coins—an amount that would pay for two months' stay in the inn. The Samaritan was prepared to pay for any other extra financial expenses. That act of attending to a robbery victim by a man who was neither a religious leader nor a Jew but a hated foreigner earned the Samaritan the title *the good Samaritan* and "the neighbour to the man who fell into the hands of robbers" (Luke 10:36). (b) In the second parable, Jesus talked about judgment that will come to all nations as they gather before him, as he sits on his throne. Like a shepherd, he will separate sheep from the goats, and put sheep on his right and goats on his left. Then he will say to those on his right:

"Come, you who are blessed by my Father; take your inheritance, the kingdom is prepared for you since the creation of the world. For I was hungry and you gave me something to eat, I was thirsty and you gave me something to drink, I was a stranger and you invited me in, I needed clothes and you clothed me, I was sick and you looked after me, I was in prison and you came to visit me." (Matt. 25:34–36)

The parable to the righteous ends with the following words that every local church needs to note, "I tell you the truth, whatever you did for one of the least of these brothers of mine, you did for me" (Matt. 25:40). Every local church has a challenge to discern the people and groups who have needs in its community, for among such needy persons, God is at work already. There are a number of things that a local church can do in its community.

First, *search for the needy.* Look for the hungry, the naked, the poor, the sick, the abandoned elderly, and other needy persons in your community. For example, as African local churches how we have responded to the following mission issues: the HIV and AIDS pandemic, violence in our communities, and poverty stricken families? I shall comment on two issues:

(a) On HIV and AIDS, it is sad to be a worshipping congregation where persons suffering from the pandemic are stigmatized as sinners who deserve punishment. The church of Christ has no other choice but to love and accept those infected by the pandemic, and to stand with the affected families. At funerals I have heard some people, including Christians, accuse other families of witchcraft when it was clear that the deceased died of AIDS. Our local churches should champion efforts to share true information about HIV and AIDS in order to dispel both superstition and fear, and teach people to love one another in spite of what the pandemic has inflicted on us. John taught, ". . . perfect love drives out fear" (1 John 4:18).

(b) There is violence everywhere—in our African villages, in the fields, on the pathways home from anywhere. There is violence in our cities—people killed in daylight, houses set on fire, and all the belongs of a family go up in smoke within minutes. Africa has developed the politics of violence everywhere. Some perpetrators of such violence may be our neighbours or fellow Christians who belong to another political party. Christians may belong to different parties, but let us not forget that we have a lot to lose if we do not look after one another the way God expects us to. Like the spies of Joshua and Rahab, the prostitute of the city of Jericho, there is a time in life when we need to look far ahead and make a binding oath, "Our lives for your lives!", in order to partake in the blessings of the promised land (Josh. 2:14), or the blessings God has prepared for us in life.

Second, *support the work of good agencies.* One day John told Jesus that he and the other disciples had come across a man who was driving out demons in Jesus' name, and that they tried to stop him because he was not part of their team. Jesus responded, "Do not stop him . . . for whoever is not against you is for you" (Luke 9:49). There are organizations in the same communities as local churches that are concerned with the control of epidemics, the purification of water, improvement of home sanitation, family care, mosquito control, nutrition instruction, and many other good things. Even though their approach may be different from ours, the local church should respect such organizations, for they are not our enemies.

One Sunday morning I listened to a pastor preach on tithing. He emphasized that the tithe was God's money and that money should never be used for any other purpose no matter how important. He mistakenly thought that God worked only through money that comes to the church, and that God had nothing to do with the rest—the nine-tenths that remains in our pockets. But all that we have belongs to God. That is the reason Paul urges the church of Corinth to give according to what one has—and to give willingly (2 Cor. 8:12). Our neighbour is the one who is hurting—the naked, the hungry, the one imprisoned unjustly, the victim of robbery. They need our neighbourliness.

At times it is essential to team with other organizations operating in our communities to carry out ministries that we may not be able to achieve alone. We also may invite professionals to share their insights with our committees in areas of communal concerns, such as education for children and public health.

Establishing a Healing and Redemptive Church

A healing and redemptive church is the seventh great mark of an evangelistic local church. A local church can impact its community by expressing and sharing the healing power of Christ in the life of their church. Often, healing ministry is misunderstood, and some Christians may feel uncomfortable when the subject of healing comes up. Jesus the Messiah brought "health and salvation."[77] Jesus perceived that connection "between his healing ministry and his redemptive ministry."[78] Hence his words, "It is not the healthy who need a doctor, but the sick.

I have not come to call the righteous, but sinners" (Mark 2:17). Jesus considered himself the redeemer and the physician of humankind. It was for that reason that the early church had an order of healers (cf. "miracles, then gifts of healing" 1 Cor. 12:28); also 12:9, where "gifts of healing", are mentioned as among the gifts of the Spirit.[79] Also, note James 5:13–16, which stresses the connection between forgiveness and healing and also mentions the anointing of the sick with oil in the name of the Lord. There is power of healing in every local church, not just for the church alone but also for the people in the entire community.

Kathy Black, Professor of Homiletics at the School of Theology at Claremont, makes a distinction between two words that are often used interchangeably—*cure* and *healing*. She describes *cure* as at least eliminating the symptoms if not the disease itself, whereas *healing* is expressed in several ways, such as in the phrases *healing presence*, *healing moment*, and *healing service*.[80] Black points out, "Each of these images elicits a sense of peace and well-being, but they do not imply cure." She goes on to say:

While a healing worship service may include hope and even prayer for a cure for a particular individual, the intent of the service is to bring some sense of well-being into the person's life, a sense of comfort, support, and peace. [For example] Linda is blind and will be physically blind for the rest of her life, but she can still experience much healing in the midst of her blindness.[81]

Black quotes John Kleich who said, ". . . healing entails finding some sense of meaning in the midst of one's situation, some sense of well-being in spite of the illness . . . healing of illness takes place always, infallibly, since everyone ultimately finds some meaning to the life situations . . ."[82] Kathy Black is a person with a disability, but she makes her position clear, "I am first and foremost a person; hence I am a '*person* with a disability.'"[83]

The distinction that Kathy Black makes between *cure* and *healing* is important. This is one of the reasons some Christians in our local churches move from one church to another. They are often seeking not healing but cure. When they see what is presented on television, which demonstrates cure, or hear of some charismatic churches that proclaim primarily cure, they become attracted to such proclamation. There is need in our local churches to show people that Christian proclamation on healing is holistic; it is both healing and redemptive to the total person. Christian understanding of healing is that it brings wholeness into all our relations, with ourselves, with neighbours, and with God. So we can plan for *healing services* in our local churches, and as Kathy Black said, "the intent of the service is to bring some sense of well-being into the person's life, a sense of comfort, support, and peace."

In 1961, Rev. Larry Eisenberg, a missionary who had recently come to Rhodesia from the United States, was appointed pastor at Ehnes Memorial Church, Old Mutare Mission. Prior to coming to Rhodesia, Larry had had some experiences with the General Board of Evangelism of The Methodist Church in Nashville, Tennessee, USA. I was also appointed an associate pastor to the same congregation from January until July 1961, when I left for studies in the United States. The first or second week of January, Larry and I talked with the leadership of Ehnes Memorial Church about holding a *healing service* on the first Thursday of the month in the evening for one hour to one and half hours in their church. At the outset, the pastor made it clear that expectations should not be focused on dramatic cases of cure from illnesses and diseases, although that was not ruled out. Rather the intent of the healing service was wholeness for individuals and for the congregation. The exhortation to the people was that they may become conscious of God's presence in our midst, and that they would present themselves to him in whatever manner the Spirit directed them.

For the five months I was present, and the period after I had gone, the results were as follows: (a) there were no dramatic cases of persons who were cured; (b) several members of Ehnes Memorial Church made remarks about a new spiritual awareness of God's presence in their lives, and an improvement in the relations between missionaries and the nationals, the authorities of the mission centre and students, and also the general labourers; and a sense of newness of spirit of fellowship by some members of the church who previously had felt they were not good enough to be members the church; and, (c) that service was beginning to draw a number of people who came from outside the Old Mutare Mission area.

I look back to that experience as a benchmark in relation to my understanding of the ministry of healing. Healing in the name of Jesus Christ in some cases may include cure, while in other cases we may have to learn from Paul's experience when the Lord said to him, "My grace is sufficient for you, for my power is made perfect in weakness" (2 Cor. 12:9). Both cure and healing are God's prerogative, and we must constantly expect anything to happen as we present ourselves and others in prayer to him. For that reason, I want to share three cases of healing—one a case shared by one of our pastors, and two out of my pastoral experiences.

As a young pastor at Chikwizo in 1960, one early morning about 6 a.m. I heard people arriving at the parsonage. Fortunately, I was already up. I opened the door, and a husband and wife came in. The husband was carrying a child in his arms, and the wife was crying, "Pastor, my child is gone!"

My immediate response was, "Let's rush to the clinic."

"No, Pastor," the husband replied, "I came here first, so that you may pray for my child."

As I took the child into my arms, I silently prayed the prayer of confession, "Lord, forgive me my unbelief." I then proceeded with an audible prayer for the sick child. As we said, "Amen" at the end of our prayer, the child was smiling at me.

The Reverend Samuel Dzobo, the former pastor of Hilltop United Methodist Church, Mutare, Zimbabwe, shared an experience of healing at Sakubva Clinic, where patients sat outside the clinic and listened to the worship service going on outdoors at Hilltop United Methodist Church. According to the testimony of the nurses, a number of patients who followed the worship were discharged a few days after, claiming healing through the message from the preachers and their participation in the worship.

In 2006, as an E. Stanley Jones Professor of Evangelism, I went to Chipfatsura United Methodist Church in Marange District on a Friday to conduct a workshop on the Two by Two Lay Visitation Evangelism Programme. I was to be there for a 7 p.m. meeting. On my way there, just as it became dark, I saw a man standing by the road. I stopped my car, and gave him a lift. He shared with me that he was going home, which was not far from where I was going. His reason for going home was that he had just received a message that his wife was seriously ill. Before he disappeared into the dark on a road that led to his home, I asked him if we could pray for his wife. As he departed, he assured me he would be home in about twenty minutes.

On the following Sunday evening, after I had returned home, I received a telephone call from the pastor of Chipfatsura United Methodist Church, telling me that man who was looking for me because he want to thank me for praying for his wife. The man said that when he got home, he found his wife awake, sitting up, and talking for the first time in three days. When the husband asked when that happened, he was told, "It was about twenty minutes ago," just as we had prayed for her.

There are a number of ways to promote the belief and practice of the ministry of healing. Every local church will have to find ways that suit its particular situation. The common denominator that all local churches share is that each is surrounded by persons who need healing in one way or another. The following are ways that some local churches have practiced the ministry of healing.

First, *an invitation to healing before either pastoral prayer or preaching.* Some pastors regularly invite people who have burdens and are weary or sick to come to the kneeling rail of the altar before the pastoral prayer. Others have a special prayer just before the pastor preaches—in response to requests from members of the congregation. Whichever way one chooses, there is a recognition of persons who may be hurting—the bereaved, those with the loved ones seriously ill, those struggling with issues of justice in society, the hungry, the homeless. This invitation recognizes Christ's presence among his people—the Christ who is ready to unburden the burdened and who gives support and acceptance to all. By invoking his presence, healing begins, enabling worshippers to participate in the worship of God in spirit and in truth. This is *healing presence*—the Lord's presence among his people, as the Prophet Isaiah experienced in the Temple and cried, "Woe to me! . . . I am ruined! For I am a man of unclean lips, . . . and my eyes have seen the King, the Lᴏʀᴅ Almighty" (Isa. 6:5). At that moment he was healed from the painful emotions of grief concerning the death of King Uzziah.

Second, *specific invitation for those seeking healing or even cure.* The pastor may extend an invitation to those members in need of healing to remain behind after the service. These persons are often invited to kneel at the altar rail, where the pastor and other leaders of the church pray for them. It is important that the pastor ask each individual who comes to kneel what concerns or problems they have. Giving the individual who is seeking healing an opportunity to unburden his/her concern is a necessary part of the healing process. It is also absolutely important for the person seeking healing to be open and honest with the pastor about his/her problem, including all that the individual has tried to do about the problem. At this point, the individual seeking healing and those making the intercessory prayer focus their faith on Christ Jesus, the Great Physician of body and spirit. At the same time they evoke the Holy Spirit to help them in their weakness, for sometimes they do not know what to say, and yet the Spirit will intercede for them (Rom. 8:26).

We should not fear failure in this ministry of healing, for it is God alone who heals his people, and not us. Ours is to believe as Christ taught his disciples, ". . . whatever you ask for in prayer, believe that you have received it, and it will be yours" (Mark 11: 24). When God has blessed your ministry with positive results, it is not something to brag or boast about. Rather, like Peter and John we also say it is the God of our ancestors, "the God of our fathers |who| has glorified his servant Jesus" (Acts 3:13). Pastors do not take pride in their own powers or reputation. Instead, we learn from the ancient priest of Israel, the Priest Eli, who said to Hannah concerning her childlessness, "Go in peace, and may the God of Israel grant you what you have asked of him" (1 Sam. 1:17).

Third, *training of the laity.* Some pastors have trained lay persons to pray for and with those in need of prayer for deliverance, exorcism, and healing. However, there are times when pastors may learn from the laity about ministry. In my first appointment at Chikwizo in Mutoko District, I came face to face with a demon-possessed person—something I had never before experienced. It was on a Sunday morning and I was preaching passionately. All of a sudden a woman came toward the altar kneeling rail, staggering as if she was drunk. I thought it was too early for anyone to respond to the message; I was still about halfway through my sermon. Immediately, I saw two women jump to their feet, lay the seemingly drunk woman on the floor, and begin to sing. The lay leader came to the pulpit and motioned me to stop preaching. I was confused until they explained what was happening. After a few minutes, an elderly, devout leader in the circuit, *Baba* Kateera, shouted, "*Buda shawi! Buda shawi!*" (Come out demon! Come out demon!). I learned about demon possession while in that circuit, and I thank God for the appointment. By the time I left that circuit, I had become a champion in exorcizing demons from those who had been tormented by them for a long time.

Fourth, *an appeal for healing of the sick*. Mainline churches today are seeing people leaving their local churches for new charismatic ones that claim to have power to heal the sick. Unfortunately, many mainline churches have avoided healing altogether, while charismatic churches regard healing purely as "cure." Television programmes on healing have made an impact on people, especially the sick. As a result, some of the sick go to charismatic pastors with their healing requests, and others fly to neighbouring countries to seek healing.

How can a local church demonstrate that it is an agent of God's healing power to individuals and the community today? Jesus had a fabulous ministry for the sick and injected new life of faith and hope in them again. He healed Simon's mother-in-law who suffered from a fever (Mark 1:29–31), he healed a man with leprosy (Mark 1:41), and many others. Similarly this power of healing was witnessed in the early church when Peter and John healed a crippled beggar (Acts 3:6ff), Paul shook off a snake into the fire without suffering any ill effects on the shore of Malta (Acts 28:1ff), and many other incidents. The power of redemption and healing is still operating in the Church of Jesus Christ. Many of us know pastors and priests in some mainline churches who have witnessed the healing power of Christ.

The people in our communities are hurting for various reasons— illness, bereaved families, family conflicts over family property due to political upheaval and natural disasters in the community, lack of justice in our nation, and indeed many other evil forces. Such persons are searching for pastors and local congregations who can provide them with healing and redemption from all these evil powers, and genuine Christian healing that will transform their total being—physical body, spirit, and social dimensions of their lives. I am aware of some pastors who already have wonderful healing ministries in their churches, and there ought to be more pastors and more mainline local churches participate in the ministry of healing for the sick.

Chapter 5

Two by Two
Lay Visitation Evangelism

One of the methods of evangelism that local churches of different denominations use is mass evangelistic meetings—often called revivals, preaching missions, crusades for souls, evangelistic campaigns, and marathons. This method of evangelism has made its contribution to the growth of the kingdom.

Another method of evangelism that has the potential to involve both full and probationary members of the local church is Two by Two Lay Visitation Evangelism (TTLVE). I used this method as a pastor, have promoted it among students in my classes at Africa University, and in local churches where I have conducted workshops. TTLVE is a method of evangelism that it is practical, that trains the laity to talk to others about their faith, and trains them for other positions in the church or community.

Jesus Calls His Disciples

First, according to Matthew 10:1, 9–14, Mark 6:6–13, and Luke 10:1–12, Jesus sends into the villages the twelve who have already been appointed and designated apostles. The twelve had been with Jesus for a while, and their time of preliminary training was over.[84] They had heard him preach and teach (Mark 4:1–34); they had witnessed his mighty works (Mark 4:35–6:6); and it was now time for them to take an active part in the ministry that Jesus was inaugurating both by words and works.[85]

Second, for Matthew and Mark, the number 12 bears a symbolic significance. It represents the twelve tribes of Israel. Matthew alone points out that Jesus instructed his disciples not to go among the Gentiles or enter any town of the Samaritans. "Go rather to the lost sheep of Israel" (Matt. 10:6), he instructed the disciples. "Twelve symbolised the new Israel since the old Israel was regarded as made up of twelve tribes" (see Matt. 19:28).[86] Therefore, the choice of twelve disciples by Matthew and Mark "was determined by the fact that their work was to be for Israel only."[87]

Like Mark and Matthew, members of a local church may want to think of their scope of mission to include those people closest to them. Often when we think of people to be visited, we overlook those closest to us, such as a spouse, parent, child, aunt, or uncle who needs to be visited for Christ's sake. For Mark and Matthew, the number 12 symbolizes localizing our evangelistic efforts; "Go rather to the lost sheep of Israel"—or to your own people (Matt.10:6, KJV).

According to Luke, Jesus "appointed seventy-two others and sent them two by two ahead of him to every town and place where he was about to go" (Luke 10:1). Luke calls them "seventy-two others, not to distinguish them from the twelve . . . but in contrast with the messengers mentioned in 9:51–52."[88] Again, the number 72 that Luke uses is symbolic. It represents the translators who produced the Septuagint version, and in the Hebrew Bible the number 70 represents the seventy nations.[89] The Gentile nations listed in Genesis 10 were reckoned by the rabbis to number 70 (or seventy-two) so that Luke regarded this mission as a symbolic anticipation of the mission to the Gentiles.[90] Thus for Luke, the sending out of the seventy-two disciples anticipated the advent of the church's mission to all the nations, including the Gentiles. That gives a local church an opportunity to think not only of closely related persons of our family and kinship, but also to make witness to Christ among our neighbours, workmates, cross-border neighbours, and to the whole world or to all nations.

Jesus Gives Authority to His Disciples

Authority in the Bible is closely connected with power, though usually distinguished from it. The word *authority* refers to the actual possession or use of power—the legal or moral right to exercise it and the domain (dominion) within which it is exercised.[91] When Jesus gave authority to his disciples over the evil spirits, he vested the same power that was exercised by prophets, priests, and by Jesus himself. It is the power that belongs absolutely to God—the power to remove the evil spirits from tormenting people. Jesus trusted the disciples to exercise such authority in the spirit of service, and not in the manner of the rulers of the Gentiles who lorded it over their subjects (Matt. 20:25).

While the disciples may have been obedient in doing everything Jesus told them to do, they did not always understand him or appreciate the mission of their Master until after the Resurrection and Pentecost. After the Resurrection the universal lordship of Christ is proclaimed (Matt. 28:18), and after Pentecost his authority is then vested in the apostles[92] and all the evangelists for building the kingdom of God on earth (2 Cor. 13:10).

The local church needs to be reminded that they share that same authority. Through the power of the Holy Spirit given to Christ's Church on the day of Pentecost, in its ministry of evangelism, evil spirits will be exorcised, the sick will be healed, the prisoners will be visited, and the oppressed will hear the good news of hope.

Jesus Instructs His Disciples

Jesus instructed his disciples on a number of things before they went out into the villages and towns. First, he instructed them what to take and what not to take with them: (Mark 6:8; Matt. 10:9–10; Luke 10:4). Second, Jesus instructed his disciples how to approach people in their homes, and that they should not expect to be received by everybody. He told them what to do when rejected by some people (Mark 6:11, Matt. 10: 11-14, Luke 10:5–7). Third, Jesus shared with his disciples the *message* for their mission in the villages and towns: (a) According to Mark, it was preaching repentance, driving out demons, and praying for and anointing the sick and healing them (Mark 6:12–13). (b) For Matthew, the message was to heal the sick, raise the dead, cleanse those who have leprosy, drive out demons, while announcing, "the kingdom of heaven is near" (Matt. 10:5–8). For Luke, it was healing the sick, and telling them "the kingdom of God is near you" (Luke 10:8–9).

From these accounts "we can learn that what the disciples were bidden to proclaim was the coming of the kingdom and that it was considered so imminent that if the news of it was to spread in time, the missionaries must travel light and not waste efforts over unreceptive audiences."[93]

Jesus Commissions His Disciples

The purpose of Jesus sending the twelve and the seventy-two disciples two by two or in pairs might have been threefold: (a) "To bolster credibility by having the testimony of more than one witness"[94] as it is written, "On the testimony of two or three witnesses a man shall be put to death, but no one shall be put to death on the testimony of only one witness" (Deut.17:6). (b) Sending out the disciples two by two provided "mutual support during their training period."[95] (c) Sending out the disciples two by two reflects the Jewish custom. For example, Jesus sent two disciples at other occasions (Mark 11:1; 14:13); John the Baptist sent two disciples to Jesus (Luke 7:18; John 1:35); the names of the apostles are presented in pairs in Matthew 10:2–4; and in Acts, Paul is paired with Barnabas and then with Silas.[96] Two disciples who were on their way to a village called Emmaus on the day that Jesus was raised from the dead when Jesus joined them in their walk, conversation, and breaking of bread (Luke 24:13ff).

Jesus Receives Reports from His Disciples

Luke alone reports the joy of the seventy-two disciples when they returned, especially that "even the demons submit to us in your name" (Luke 10:17). There are two points to consider about this report.

First, while the disciples were away, busy exorcising demons from people,

> Jesus has one of his ecstatic experiences, this time a vision of Satan falling from heaven. The vision is prophetic: the exorcisms of Jesus and his disciples were not themselves the decisive victory over Satan, but only tokens of a victory yet to be won through the Cross . . . Up to this point, it should be noted, Satan is still in heaven . . . (Job 1; Zech. 3:1–5) . . . The ejection of Satan means that God's redemptive mercy has delivered men both from the sentence that hung over them and from the guilt and power of sin that held the captive. (Rev. 7–12)[97]

It was a great success that the disciples were able to exorcise demons from those who had suffered untold torments from such evil powers. Further, it "was the earthly success of the disciples that occasioned Jesus' vision of a heavenly triumph."[98] In other words, the accomplishment of Jesus, including his work through the disciples on earth is a good sign that Satan's dominion over the people has been broken down.[99]

Second, having supported the success of the mission, Jesus cautioned the disciples to understand that "the real ground for rejoicing"[100] was that their "names are written in heaven" (Luke 10:20; cf. Exod. 32:32–33; Ps. 69:28; Dan. 12:1; Enoch 104:1; Rev. 3:5).

Advantages of Using Two by Two Lay Visitation Evangelism

TTLVE is a method of evangelism that every local church, circuit, or parish needs to try. There are the several advantages of using two-by-two mode for evangelism.

First, for those who voluntarily go for training and are willingly sent out to witness:

a. It is a method of evangelism that provides mutual support for all in the lay visitation evangelism programme, especially for beginners.
b. It is a good way of training oneself in personal evangelism, and in taking other positions of responsibility in the congregation and community.
c. It bolsters credibility by having a testimony of more than one witness.

Second, for the community:

a. It ensures that every member or family of the community that needs to be visited by somebody is visited.
b. It is focused on finding and visiting people at home, and it can also be extended to other places, such as nursing homes, hospitals and clinics, prisons, and workplaces.
c. It prompts a new awareness within the local church about the conditions under which the people in the community are living.

Third, for the local church:

a. It brings the church face to face with the world and the basic needs of people, such as a sense of belonging, food, shelter, and clean water. These needs that people face in their community direct God's mission for the local church.
b. It enables members of the church to hear the story of individuals in their community and to learn about them, their needs, fears, aspirations, and what they think about Christians and the church.
c. It enables the church to minister to people in their homes or wherever they are found, and it may also open doors to subsequent visits for ministry. There are many persons in our communities who live alone and who would love being visited by someone.
d. It is a method of evangelism that can involve every member of the local church in the work. There are no spectators. It does not

require special gifts in any way. It does not mean that every member of the local church is forced to participate in the visitation. Rather, it means there is an opportunity for every member who wishes to participate in the programme to do so. The pastor should always begin with volunteers. Members who are not able to participate in the programme, such as the elderly, persons with disabilities, or those with work commitments that conflict with the time of the programme, can always support the programme through other means. For example, people with disability and elderly members who may have difficulties in travelling far distances may form prayer groups where they pray for those who are sent out by the church. Members whose work commitments conflict with the visitation programme can pray as well as giving additional monetary or other means to support the visitation programme. Those who are hesitant to go out and visit can always be part of the praying group. But every member of the church can be involved in the programme in one way or another. Jerome is quoted as saying, "Baptism is the ordination of the laity,"[101] meaning every one who has been baptized has been ordained an evangelist. I would add that every convert to Christ becomes an evangelist.

e. It ensures tangible results by bringing renewal in the church and often by increasing church membership.

Commissioning Members of the Local Church

Jesus used private conversation and visits extensively as ways of doing evangelism. We can all learn from him on how to talk about God to others. As much as Jesus spoke to crowds of people in synagogues, temple courts, on the mountainside, and at the seaside, still he took time to visit with and talk to people about their lives and their needs wherever he found them. Today there are local churches that engage in the lay visitation evangelism programme—"modeled after Jesus' training his disciples and sending them out in pairs."[102] Let us examine together what needs to be done in order for members of a local church to engage in such a programme.

First, members of the local church can be commissioned by the pastor and congregation to go out into the community. Barnabas and Paul were commissioned by their local church in Antioch before leaving on their first missionary journey (Acts 13:3).

Second, the participants in the TTLVE programme need instruction before they are sent out into the community. Two lessons are given: (a) a lesson on how Jesus sent out his disciples using the biblical texts mentioned above; and (b) a lesson on basic skills, such as how to start a conversation with the person you are visiting (see John 4:7), learning to do more listening and less talking, and paying "close attention to life events and turning points,"[103]

Third, the pastor with the assistance of the lay leader commissions the participants in the lay visitation programme and sends them off with a prayer. That commissioning gives them the authority for the church's mission. The participants are taught to introduce themselves to the people they are visiting as following:

> I am Mrs. Makura, and my colleague is Mr. Muti. We are members of St. Paul United Methodist Church, here in town or village. Our pastor, the Reverend Tendai Matota, and our congregation, St. Paul, have sent us to pay you a visit this afternoon.

Fourth, as the lay visitors or evangelists approach the people in the community or homes, they may find themselves in any one of three categories:

a. *Evangelistic visiting*: a visit where the two visitors realize the family or individual they are visiting is a non-believer in Christ. They do not know Christ, or have not heard or accepted him as their

Saviour or Lord of their life. Therefore, the visitors' task is to "offer Christ" to them—to introduce them to Jesus Christ.

b. *Friendly visiting*: a visit to a person who knows something about Christ or the church. Although this person may have backslidden from the faith, do not approach them as a heathen. Approach him or her as one who knows better. These persons need a listening ear, rather than to hear only the visitors talking. Often such persons hurt and they may have a lot to say about the church, Christians, the pastor, or his/her predecessor. Above all, they need someone they believe understands them. Offer Christ as a friend to them—a friend because they already know what you offer them. If such a person is a backslider from your church, and you happen to remember what good things the individual used to do, remind the person about it, and make him or her feel he or she is missed. At all cost, avoid arguments.

c. *Shut-in visiting*: a visit to the elderly, the disabled, the sick, in their home, a home for the elderly, or hospital. Often, these persons are unable to come to church and worship with others. These are people who may demand a lot of your time. They want to talk and share what they are missing by not coming to church. Again, spend time listening to them rather than doing all the talking. They may even ask you to sing their favourite hymn with them. Often, people found in shut-in situations have serious needs or concerns—for shelter, health, food, or company. They need to be ministered to right then. A report should be made to the church to try and meet their needs. They may feel lonely. Even when they are looked after by a son or and daughter, who may be working, they may complain about this and that. Again, the best ministry to them is to be good listeners.

Fifth, all the participants in the two by two lay visitation programme are sent out primarily to share the love of God through word and deed—to share by word of mouth and to minister to those who may be shut-ins for whatever reason. If from the above accounts "we can learn that what the disciples were bidden to proclaim was the coming of the kingdom and that it was considered so imminent that if the news of it was to spread in time, the missionaries must travel light and not waste efforts over unreceptive audiences,"[104] likewise, it is urgent for us to spread the good news to many who need God's gracious love.

The Local Church Receives Reports

The most rewarding part of the TTLV programme is the return of the participants as they give reports of their visits. Listening to group reports is so exciting and elating that some participants break down with emotion and amazement. Such reports are the source of great testimonies, both by those who are obedient to being sent out, and those who are visited at a time when they thought no one was concerned about them.

The following reports are examples of what happened on five visits, but the names of the visitors and churches have been changed.

First, Mrs. Kute and Mrs. Kufa paid a friendly visit to Mrs. Musi, who had abruptly stopped coming to church on Sundays or to any other church meetings. After the two visitors introduced themselves, and shared the message that they had been sent by Pastor Pute and the congregation that Mrs. Musi had been a member of for many years, Mrs. Musi replied, "This is my church that I used to know—the church that cares for its members. But let me ask you some questions: You come to see me now! When my daughter gave birth, no one from my church came to see us. Was it because the child was an illegitimate child? We had death in the family, and no one came. Why are you coming now?" After some discussion, she seemed to have changed her mind. "Anyway, I want to thank the new pastor. By the way, what is her name again? Since we are still remembered, I plan to be in church tomorrow, on Sunday." Of the twenty-two persons who were visited that Saturday afternoon, Mrs. Musi was one of the ten who attended the Sunday worship service with us the following day.

Second, Mrs. Toto and Mrs. Zuze paid an evangelistic visit to Mr. and Mrs. Zengeni—an elderly couple. According to the two visitors, neither Mr. nor Mrs. Zengeni looked well. But Mr. Zengeni was quite conversant. As the conversation went on, Mr. Zengeni became more open to his visitors. "I am a decent old man," he said. "I do not go to church as much as I would want to. I have no problems with anyone in the community; I do not beat my wife. She has often urged that we come to your church, but I have been reluctant. The reason for my reluctance is that I have a problem with tobacco. I smoke. I admit that smoking is a bad habit, and I know your church does not want people who smoke. I cannot even think of going to any other church because they are all too far for us to walk there," said Mr. Zengeni.

The two evangelistic visitors assured Mr. Zengeni that tobacco should not stand between him and God. The two, not knowing exactly how to proceed, urged Mr. Zengeni to come to church and plan to commit himself as a member of the church. They assured him that the pastor would assist him concerning his problem with tobacco, and more especially about his membership. Mr. Zengeni seemed relieved with that advice, and with the invitation to come to church. To their surprise, Mr. Zengeni asked the two visitors to sing for him *Mwari Mubatsiri Wedu* (God Is Our Helper). After singing, they prayed with the couple.

Third, two youths, Grace and Thomas, paid an evangelistic visit to Mr. and Mrs. Potsa. That was not the first time the couple had been approached by members of this particular church. As soon as the two young visitors arrived, Mrs. Potsa asked: "Have you come to invite us to church?"

"Yes!" the young visitors responded. "Our pastor, Reverend Farai, and our congregation at Mukute Church sent us to pay you a visit this afternoon."

Mrs. Potsa then turned to her husband and said, "You know Mr. Potsa, I have always wanted to turn a new leaf. I have been thinking of going to church lately."

The husband looked surprised and impressed. Mrs. Potsa told the two young visitors, "I will come to church next Sunday." Later, the pastor confirmed that she came to church that following Sunday.

Fourth, Mrs. Tiko and Mrs. Susa paid a visit to Mrs. Gobe. This elderly lady, a shut-in, was a member of the church. She lived alone. Mrs. Gobe is now unable to walk to church because of sore feet and old age. After Mrs. Gobe had been told that the two visitors were sent by the pastor, Mr. Tote, and the congregation at Mutondo Church to pay a visit with her that afternoon, she was very pleased. In their observation, "She became lively once more!" Immediately, Mrs. Gobe said to the visitors, "Please, don't you say anything; I want you to listen to me." She complained about many things, including her sore feet, loneliness, sleepless nights, and deaths in the family. She felt that many of those things happening around her were affecting her devotion to prayerful life. After sharing all this with the visitors, Mrs. Gobe thanked the pastor and her congregation for remembering her. The two visitors cleaned Mrs. Gobe's house and blankets, prepared a meal for her, and saw to it that she ate her meal before they returned to the church for the reports service. After the church received the report that evening, they took a special offering, and the following day the two visitors were sent with money to assist Mrs. Gobe.

Fifth, Mrs. Soko and Mr. Shumba visited Mrs. Mbada, a single mother. Unfortunately, she was not at home. They left a note to say they were coming back late that afternoon. Upon their return, they found Mrs. Soko at home. She welcomed her two visitors warmly, wondering what had caused their visit. As soon as the visitors introduced themselves, Mrs. Soko responded, "Since my first son died two years ago, I have not attended church. What disappointed me was that no one from my church came to see me, neither did I receive any assistance from the church. As far as I am concerned, my political party is my saviour. They helped with everything, and so every Sunday I go to their meetings."

While they listened to Mrs. Soko, the latter's sister, Mrs. Tsuro, who belongs to one of the churches in the community arrived. In joining the conversation, Mrs. Tsuro indicated that she was a cross-border trader, who one Sunday was successful in persuading her husband to go to church with her. "What was most disappointing was the message the preacher delivered that morning. It was all about how women who cross borders are misbehaving. As far as that preacher is concerned, all cross-border women traders misbehave. Both my husband and I have never gone back to my church again, and I cannot convince him to go back to church and listen to that kind of preaching." The two visitors tried to assure the two ladies that things were changing, but in vain. What the two visitors, Mrs. Soko and Mr.Shumba, shared with the rest of the congregation that evening was, "It is good to listen to what people outside there think of us."

Listening to such reports is exciting, and brings renewal to the soul. Again, the real grounds for the joy that comes out of this experience is not what the individual has achieved, rather it is the awareness and the assurance that one is in God's hands and one is in the presence of God—and that one's name is written in heaven.

Chapter 6

Planning an Evangelism Programme

There are ten points that may be helpful in planning an evangelism programme for the local church. The points are meant to be guidelines only, rather than the ten commandments.

Need for the Evangelism Committee

In order to have an effective and lasting programme of evangelism, it is important that the local church has a committee on evangelism, or its equivalent. Various denominations have different structures for the same ministries in their local churches, and it is through the committee on evangelism that the local church is efficiently mobilised for the ministry of evangelism.

Vision for the Evangelistic Task

Once the committee on evangelism is in place it takes responsibility to plan evangelistic programmes for its local church or circuit. The committee needs to have a vision of what is to be accomplished by its church in the community. That vision may come either from the pastor, the laity of the local church, or members of the committee. It is the responsibility of the committee to make sure all members of the church catch the vision that it promotes. The Bible teaches, "Where there is no vision, the people perish" (Prov. 29:18 KJV). That means the pastor, the committee on evangelism, and the local church all need to be visionary in their perception and planning for the ministry of evangelism.

A vision is the ability to perceive the future through what is given to a person in the present; or the ability to perceive the potential in any given enterprise; or the mental image of what the future holds. As believers, we often consider such insight God-given, for even God is understood as having such visions: "Let us make man in our image, after our likeness" (Gen. 1:26, KJV). Every great success begins with a vision or great imagination. Hence the saying, "Change your thoughts—change your life. . . A man is what he thinks about all day long. . . If you will change your thinking, you will change your life. . . If you only care enough for a result you will almost certainly obtain it."[105] It all depends on the vision one has in life. That vision may not come easily. One may have to wait for it for a long time (Hab. 2:3), and when it does come, it may be costly. It was his vision of a new humanity that sent Jesus of Nazareth to hang on the cross as a Roman criminal. Yes, he sustained a vision of a people who would be victorious over their arch-enemy, namely death, after his resurrection. Hence, Paul in proclaiming the Resurrection of Jesus cries out, "Where, O death, is your victory? Where, O death, is your sting?" (1 Cor. 15:55). Through the Resurrection of Jesus Christ, who was raised by God the Father, both sin, the sting of death, and death itself have been conquered, and Christ shares that victory with those who believe in him (1 Cor. 15:54–57). It cost Nelson Mandela twenty-seven years on Robben Island to keep a vision of South Africa liberated from apartheid. A vision is all about the future, and of what we can become, or what a country, organization, local church, or congregation, can become.

Mission Statement

A vision that a church has for its evangelistic ministry needs to be developed into a mission statement. The mission statement expresses the following points: (a) the evangelistic task the local church intends accomplishing in its community; and (b) the methodology it proposes to follow in achieving the evangelistic mission. The purpose of the mission statement is to bring into focus and clarify the church's evangelistic intentions.

Penhalonga Circuit expresses its vision in this mission statement: "To reach out to the mine employees, their families, and all other dwellers in the mining village with the purpose of making them Christian disciples by introducing them to the gospel of Jesus Christ, guiding them in their growth toward its fulfilment in their lives, and equipping such disciples for continuous evangelistic ministry of the church through periodical lay training programmes."

Assess the Strength of the Local Church or Circuit

After the committee on evangelism has developed its mission statement, which gives a clear picture of the task to be done, it is important that the local church now assess its own strength or resources. Jesus taught his disciples:

> Or suppose a king is about to go to war against another king. Will he not first sit down and consider whether he is able with ten thousand men to oppose the one coming against him with twenty thousand? (Luke 14:31)

This is the time for the committee on evangelism to ask the following questions: What methods of evangelism should the local church use in their situation? A programme of evangelism for the whole year may include the use of various methods of sharing the gospel to different groups of people in the community. The committee may consider methods such as personal evangelism, two-by-two lay visitation evangelism, or mass evangelistic meetings. The committee may also ask itself the following questions: Do we need outside help? What resources do we have or lack? How much time do we need for training the whole church? What are the target groups for the evangelistic programme? Do we have the personnel to launch the programme? What is the duration of our campaign—one day, one week, one month, six months, or twelve months? Responses to all these questions need careful thought and planning.

Setting Goals

Any local church or circuit wants to see a membership of committed believers that is growing numerically and maturing in their understanding of Christian discipleship. For that to happen, the local church will need to set some goals regarding their evangelistic programme. Or they may need to set some targets for themselves. They may want to decide how many people they hope to reach out to or visit in a given time. Many churches are not used to setting goals for themselves, and yet they may be involved in lots of evangelistic activities. Indeed, numbers of committed believers may be on the increase in the life of a congregation—even without setting any goals. However, not setting goals is like going on a journey without stating your destination. How do you know where you are headed?

The advantages of setting goals for evangelistic programmes are as follows: (a) Goals clarify the mission of the evangelistic task. As a young boy growing up in a village, I went hunting with older men of the village from time to time. The first game that we killed was lifted up for all the dogs to see and sniff it. It was believed that allowing the dogs to sniff the first kill would make them sense the purpose of hunting. Setting goals in our evangelistic ministry is lifting targets that we wish to attain. Let the members "sniff" or understand them. (b) Setting goals encourages members of the church to persevere. Paul talks of perseverance when he says, "Forgetting what is behind and straining toward what is ahead, I press on toward the goal to win the prize for which God has called me heavenward in Christ Jesus" (Phil. 3:13–14). He had his goal before him. Good goals in our evangelistic planning become a challenge that brings out the best of faith in God's people, as well as their dependence upon God's power. (c) Goals enable believers to evaluate the programme at the end. It does not help much to evaluate your programme without prior setting of goals. The practice of setting goals applies to both short period evangelistic campaigns and long-term campaigns.

Again, goals of an evangelistic programme should not be set for converts to be won; rather, goals may be set for the number of people or homes to be visited or reached by a local church. The issue of converts remains God's prerogative—at his own time.

Approval of the Programme

To assure the success of an evangelistic programme in the local church, it should be approved through normal channels of the church. This also enables the whole church to become aware of the programme in as much detail as possible. We need to take all the necessary steps as required by the regulations of our church when organising anything. Further, we needs to minimise friction especially when with those members in the congregation who may have different views about evangelism. By presenting the programme to the church body through the normal channels for approval, the committee on evangelism informs people and emphasises that the support of the programme by all members is important for its success.

Action Plan

The committee on evangelism is responsible for creating the action plan. Once the programme has been approved, it becomes the official evangelism programme of the local church or circuit. The next step is for the committee on evangelism to mobilise the whole church in implementing it. At this point, the committee will need to develop an action plan. Often the action plan calls for members of the local church to do different things. The committee should use volunteers as much as possible. Allow people to serve where they think they would make their best contribution to the success of the programme. As much as one would want to see the whole church involved, there may be a few people who are hesitant. Avoid forcing anyone to participate, but leave the door open for those people who may change their minds later.

There are a number of ways to involve members of a local church, which could include nearly everyone.

Planning an evangelistic campaign in the life of the church is a big challenge that has to be met with everything the congregation has at its disposal. Some members of the church may begin to realise the importance of prayer in their life. This could prove to be an opportunity for the pastor to teach the laity to pray for the power of the Holy Spirit in their church as they become involved in the programme. This may be the chance to teach people to understand the importance of praying for the leadership of their church—the pastor, lay leadership, the committee on evangelism, the community, the people and homes they hope to visit, the nation, and concerns that the members may have. The elderly persons and those with a physical disability, who may not be able to do what the other members do, can always be organised to meet either at the church or at another convenient place to offer prayer support. This does not make the ministry of prayer a secondary option; rather, the ministry of prayer is a priority. We are always reminded of the Twelve, who decided to delegate administrative responsibilities to others, while they paid attention "to prayer and the ministry of the word" (Acts 6:4). An evangelism programme of this nature and magnitude often provides the church with an opportunity to promote prayer life in the whole local church or circuit by organising prayer cells. The church could promote family prayer cells, business prayer cells, neighbourhood cells, and various church cells—such as sections, church member to church member prayer cells, and many others. However, the focus is to pray for the evangelistic activities.

Planning for an evangelistic programme provides an opportunity to the local church to organise Bible study groups. If the church already has such groups, they will be revitalised. If not, an evangelistic programme may provide the church with the opportunity to start Bible study for those who wish to do so. It might be a good time to study a book of the Bible, such as Acts 1:1 through 19:20. The church may choose to study the birth of the Church (Acts 1:1–5:2), the beginnings of Gentile Christianity (9:32–12:25), Paul's first missionary journey and the Apostolic decree, (13:1–16:5), or the evangelization of the Aegean shores (16:6–19:20). The committee could recommend the study of one of the Gospels, or an Old Testament book that relates well to the evangelistic programme. Such study of the Bible related to the evangelistic mission of the local church is likely to bear lasting results in the life of the church.

This is the time to ask: Who will do what during the course of the evangelistic campaign? If there are guest preachers to be invited, this is the time for them to be identified. Or, the committee may decide to have their pastor as their evangelist.

If the local church or circuit intends to include the TTLV mode for evangelism, the committee will have to identify persons and homes that church members plan to visit in the community. Handling of names of the persons who are to be visited in the community is a delicate issue, and should be done with great care. This is one area of planning where the pastor needs to train his or her members. Further, this is where members of the church need to be taught that praying for such persons in their gathering is a conversation between the church and God, and not between the members themselves. What members petition or intercede in prayer to their heavenly Father should not become a subject of talk or gossip. Failure to understand these things may spoil the evangelistic programme.

Organizing Training

The pastor should organise training programmes for the whole church. Generally speaking, the church members are interested in evangelism. It may be possible that some people who may want to participate in an evangelistic programme may not have a clear understanding of what evangelism is. Some may not be interested in what they have witnessed about evangelism. Many others tend to shy away until they are assured that there is training available. Some people may be eager to reach out to others but lack training on how to approach people or talk to people. Of course, there are those who think evangelism is only for pastors and those who are gifted for the ministry. A local church can do a lot in the training of its members for the ministry of evangelism. Just as there are many ways of doing evangelism, there are also many ways of training members of the church to be involved in evangelism.

There is a sense in which the laity can learn to be evangelists by imitating their pastor. That could be one point to begin to understand what the ministry of evangelism is about. In writing to the church of Thessalonica, Paul says, "You know how we lived among you for your sake. You became imitators of us and of the Lord" (1 Thess. 1:5–6).

> It had cost, and was still costing, these Thessalonians something to become Christians and to maintain their Christian lives among their fellows (2:14; 3:2–5, 7; II Thess. 1:4). It had cost Paul and his associates to become Christians and to be Christian evangelists (2:2, 15–16; 3:7), just as it had cost the Lord Jesus to carry forward his ministry.[106]

The way the pastor pays attention to his or her prayer life and Bible study, to caring for every member of the Lord's flock, developing and preaching evangelistic sermons, and conducting himself or herself as an evangelist is in itself a great lesson about evangelism to church members. That is what makes members of the church want to become imitators of their pastor and the Lord.

The pastor may need to train people on how to handle demon exorcism. But in some churches, the members may need to teach young and inexperienced pastors who have not experienced persons possessed by demons. This was true for me. As I related earlier, as I preached in the main church of my circuit on a Sunday morning, during my first appointment as a young pastor, a woman stood up and screamed with a loud voice and suddenly fell on the floor. I was shocked, and was not sure what was happening. As I tried to continue with my sermon, one of the laypersons asked me to stop preaching. Within a short time the elderly members of the church surrounded the woman who was possessed, keeping her under control, while the whole church sang a hymn, clapping their hands, with others kneeling down in prayer. That was my first encounter with a demon-possessed person. In that first appointment of my ministerial career, I learned a lot from laypeople of my circuit about how to deal with people who sought deliverance "from the dominion of darkness" in order to be led "into the kingdom of the Son" of God (Col. 1:13). This is a part of African life—its belief and practice—which the African pastor or leaders cannot avoid.

Dealing with demon exorcism is not respectable practice in some quarters. It appears that *exorcism* is a word that some pastors would rather ignore. Consequently, some African pastors either keep silent about it or use some other more polished and respectable term. This is what Max Assimeng, a professor of sociology, said, "Things are truer if un-African, so we quote Americans. It is traditional, but projected in modern dress. The more foreign, the more serious, true, powerful it is."[107] It is for this reason that as appalling as some aspect of our old traditional culture may be, it is part of us. It is deadly and we have many of our people who are still deeply entrenched in that kind of life, who need the good news of Jesus Christ so that they are led to new life and the fullness of life in Jesus Christ.

The pastor can train the laity by helping them become aware of the social problems that people are facing in their communities. There are some people who believe that the church is not relevant to them in this life because it is too pre-occupied with heaven. As we read about the ministry of Jesus in the Gospels, it dawns on us that people with all

kinds of problems—personal and social, religious and cultural, economic and political—constantly surrounded him. These people did
not come to him at the temple or synagogue. Rather, Jesus went to
where these people were to be found and he ministered to them where
they were.

To his fellow believers, the Jews, Jesus told stories, such as that of
the rich man and Lazarus (Luke 16:19–31)—a story in which the latter
was constantly ignored by the former. Jesus was talking about his con-
temporary society, which ignored many "Lazaruses." Hence, his ministry leaned toward the disadvantaged—the poor, sinners, tax collectors,
women, children, the demon possessed, lepers, the lame, blind, and
deaf. Anyone who had a disability, in fact, was forbidden by law to make
offering or go near the altar (Lev. 21:17–23).

No wonder when the Son of Man comes in his glory he will say, "I
tell you the truth, whatever you did for one of the least of these brothers of mine, you did for me" (Matt. 25:40). This approach to the ministry of evangelism needs serious attention by the Church in Africa. It
teaches us that the essence of evangelism is not merely a matter of
piety. Rather, obedience and faithfulness to a people-oriented ministry is what Jesus demonstrated during his three-year ministry in Galilee and Judea. Evangelism should be concerned about new political
developments, about "national government unity" that African nations
adopt, and about the ever-increasing exploitation of African's natural
resources by our so-called friends and by some of our African governments. Evangelism points to Jesus as the good news because we all
want to experience real life in all its fullness (John 10:10) in Christ, now
and forever.

Select the Day to Launch the Programme

Regardless of the method or methods of evangelism that the local
church decides to use, there must be a day when all members celebrate the launching of the programme. The launch can be marked by

a special worship service, which may include commissioning of every member or all who will be participating in the programme. It will also mean a special message from the pastor to give direction and meaning to the whole programme.

Evaluate the Results

Whether the duration of the evangelistic campaign is short and long, the committee on evangelism should always evaluate the results of their work. Obviously, the church will want to know if they were faithful to their commitments or successful in fulfilling their goals. There is always need to reassess all the ten steps, and make adjustments where necessary. Above all, such an exercise should create a sense of mission—awareness of the life of the whole church. The local church may begin to realise that they are both a church gathered and a church scattered. They are gathered every Sunday for worship, and during weekdays they are scattered over the whole community for their livelihood work and witness.

After the evaluation of the results, the local church or circuit needs to give thanks and celebrate the victories in Christ. Often, when a church has started a programme of evangelism in its life, there is no end to it. It means it is prepared to proclaim and share the good news "in season and out of season" (2 Tim. 4:2). We may change ways of doing the ministry of evangelism, but never graduate members from the task of evangelism. We must therefore, celebrate all the time. For any local church or circuit to "rejoice in the Lord always" (Phil. 4:4) as Paul commands, the church needs to remain involved in the ministry of evangelism all the time.

Endnotes

1. *The Book of Discipline of The United Methodist Church* 2004 (Nashville: Abingdon Press, 2004), 127.
2. W. R. F. Browning, A *Dictionary of the Bible* (1996), 76.
3. Ibid.
4. Ibid.
5. Kenneth Scott Latourette, A *History of Christianity* (1953), 132.
6. Ibid., 356.
7. Ibid., 525.
8. Nolan B. Harmon, *Understanding the Methodist Church* (1955), 102.
9. Rupert E. Davis, *Methodism* (1963), 89.
10. Ibid.
11. Ibid.
12. Ibid.
13. *The Book of Discipline of The United Methodist Church* 2004, 127.
14. Bryan Green, *The Practice of Evangelism* (New York: Charles Scribner's Sons, 1951), 46.
15. *The Book of Discipline of the* UMC 2004, #215, 135.
16. *The Book of Discipline of the* UMC, *Africa Central Conference ed.* (1990), #104, 49.
17. Barclay M. Newman, A *Concise Greek-English Dictionary of the New Testament* (London: United Bible Societies, 1971), 75.
18. Roberto Escamilla, *Come To the Feast* (Nashville: Broadman & Holman Publishers, 1998), 9.
19. Dana L. Robert, *Evangelism as the Heart of Mission* (New York: General Board of Global Ministries of the UMC, 1997), 1ff.
20. Alva I. Cox, *Christian Education in the Church Today* (Nashville: Graded Press, 1965), 35.
21. Walter, Klaiber, *Call and Response* (Nashville: Abingdon Press, 1997), 15.
22. Ibid.
23. Gerald H. Anderson & Thomas F. Stransky, C.S.P., *Mission Trends No. 2—Evangelization* (New York: Paulist Press, 1975), 9.
24. Ibid.
25. Ibid.
26. Klaiber, *Call & Response*, 15.
27. Ibid.
28. Jean-Jacques van Allmen, *Preaching and Congregation* (Richmond: John Knox Press, 1962), 7.

29. Van A. Harvey, A *Handbook of Theological Terms* (1964), 190.
30. Ibid.
31. F. F. Bruce, *Commentary on the Book of the Acts* (1966), 194.
32. G. Abbott-Smith, A *Manual Greek Lexicon of the New Testament* (1968), 249.
33. W. E. Vine, *An Expository Dictionary of New Testament Words*, Vol I, (1966), 163.
34. George H. Hunter, *Church for the Unchurched* (1996), 9.
35. Kenneth Scott Latourette, A *History of Christianity* (New York: Harper & Row, Publishers, 1953), 85.
36. Latourette, A *History of Christianity*, 211.
37. Williston Walker, A *History of the Christian Church* (New York: Charles Scribner's Sons, 1959), 101.
38. Samuel Laeuchli, *The Serpent and the Dove* (Nashville: Abingdon Press, 1966), 22.
39. Latourette, A *History of Christianity*, 211f.
40. Reignhold Seeberg, *History of Doctrines in the Ancient Church*, Vol. I, (1964), 141.
41. Howard Grimes, *The Rebirth of the Laity*, 46. *Constitution of the Holy Apostles and James Donaldson* (1899), VII, 404, 410.
42. Ibid.
43. Hendrik Kraemer, A *Theology of the Laity* (1958), 17.
44. Ibid., 48.
45. Kraemer, A *Theology of the Laity*, 53.
46. Tony Lane, *Christian Thought* (1984), 26.
47. Clyde L. Manschreck, A *History of Christianity* (Englewood Cliffs, N.J: Prentice-Hall, 1964), 19.
48. Ibid.
49. Ibid., 20.
50. Ibid., 19.
51. Harvey, A *Handbook of Theological Terms* (1964), 190.
52. Clyde L. Manschreck, A *History of Christianity*, 271.
53. Ibid., 273.
54. Ibid., 268.
55. Manschreck, A *History of Christianity*, 268f.
56. Manschreck, A *History of Christianity*, 273.
57. Georgia Harkness, *The Church and Its Laity* (1962), 70.
58. Ibid., 71.
59. Theodore H. Robinson, *The Moffatt Commentary of Matthew* (New York: Harper & Row, 1927), 236.
60. James S. Stewart, *Heralds of God* (New York: Charles Scribner's Sons, 1946), 61.
61. Merrill R. Abbey, *Living Doctrine in a Vital Pulpit* (Nashville: Abingdon Press, 1964), 30.
62. J. F. Bethune-Baker, *An Introduction to the Early History of Christian Doctrine* (London: Methuen & Co., Ltd., 1949), 1.
63. Dennis Kimbro and Napoleon Hill, *Think and Grow Rich* (New York: Fawcett Crest, 1991), 125.

64. W. E. Sangster, *The Craft of Sermon Construction* (Philadelphia: Westminster Press, 1951), 53.
65. Gordon Pratt Baker and Edward Ferguson, Jr., eds., "How to Give an Altar Call in a Local Church," *A Year of Evangelism in the Local Church* (Nashville: Tidings Materials for Christian Evangelism, 1960), 72.
66. W. R. F. Browning, *A Dictionary of the Bible* (Oxford: Oxford University Press, 1996), 13.
67. Alan Richardson, ed., *A Theological Word Book of the Bible* (New York: The MacMillan Company, 1950), 209.
68. Browning, *A Dictionary of the Bible*, 13.
69. *The Financial Gazette* (2–8 December 2010), A3–A5.
70. Harrell F. Beck, *Our Biblical Heritage* (Boston: United Church Press, 1964), 2.
71. Dwight E. Stevenson, *In the Biblical Preacher's Workshop* (Nashville: Abingdon Press, 1967), 18.
72. Davies, *Methodism*, 73.
73. *Foundations: Sharing the Ministry of Christian Education in Your Congregation* (1993), 4.
74. Cullmann, *Prayer in The New Testament*, 17.
75. W. E. Sangster, *Teach Me to Pray* (1959), 36f.
76. Thomas D. Blakely, Walter E. A. van Beek and Dennis L. Thomson, eds., *Religion in Africa* (London: James Currey, 1994), 280.
77. Alan Richardson, ed., *A Theological Word Book of the Bible* (1950), 103.
78. Ibid.
79. Ibid.
80. Kathy Black, *A Healing Homiletic* (Nashville: Abingdon Press, 1996), 51.
81. Ibid.
82. Ibid.
83. Ibid., 17.
84. C. E. B. Cranfield, *The Gospel According to St. Mark* (Cambridge: The University of Cambridge, 1963), 199.
85. D. E. Nineham, *Saint Mark* (London: Penguin Books, 1992), 167.
86. *Oxford Dictionary of the Bible* (Oxford: Oxford University Press, 1996), 380.
87. Alan Richardson, ed., *A Theological Word Book of the Bible* (New York: The Macmillan Company,1950), 271.
88. G. B. Caird, *The Gospel of St. Luke* (London: Penguin Books, 1968) 144.
89. William Manson, *The Gospel of Luke* (New York: Harper and Brothers Publishers (1930), 123.
90. G. B. Caird, *The Gospel of St. Luke* (London: Penguin Books, 1963), 144.
91. *The Interpreter's Dictionary of the Bible*, Vol. A–D (Nashville: Abingdon Press, 1962), 319.
92. *Oxford Dictionary of the Bible*, 30f.
93. Nineham, *The Gospel of Saint Mark*, 169.
94. Kenneth Baker, ed., *The NIV Study Bible* (Grand Rapids: Zondervan Publishing House, 1995), 1502.
95. Ibid.

96. C. E. B. Cranfield, *The Gospel According to Mark* (Cambridge: Cambridge University Press, 1963).
97. G. B. Caird, *The Gospel of St. Luke*, 143.
98. Ibid.
99. Ibid.
100. *The Interpreter's Bible*, Vol. 8, 189.
101. George E. Sweazey, *Effective Evangelism* (New York: Harper & Brothers, 1953), 89ff.
102. Clinton M. Marsh, *Evangelism Is . . .* (Louisville: Geneva Press, 1997), 5.
103. Hanchey, *Church Growth and the Power of Evangelism*, 62.
104. Nineham, *Saint Mark*, 169.
105. Dennis Kimbro and Napoleon Hill, *Think and Grow Rich* (New York: Fawcett Crest, 1991), 33.
106. *The Interpreter's Bible*, Vol. 11 (Nashville: Abingdon Press, 1955), 262.
107. Paul Gifford, *African Christianity* (Bloomington: Indiana University Press), 102.

CPSIA information can be obtained
at www.ICGtesting.com
Printed in the USA
FSOW01n0420220117
29879FS